THE ULTIMATE
IRISH CHALLENGE

SAYINGS, HISTORY AND ABSURDITIES
ABOUT IRELAND AND THE IRISH PEOPLE

BILL O'NEILL

ISBN: 978-1-64845-131-7

DON'T FORGET
YOUR FREE BOOK

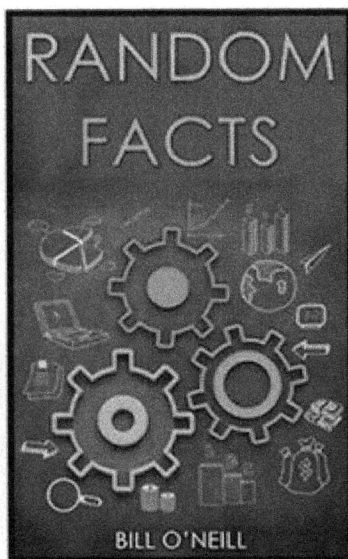

GET THEM FOR FREE ON
WWW.TRIVIABILL.COM

CONTENTS

INTRODUCTION

How Irish are you?

A great many Americans claim to have Irish blood in their veins and will happily wax lyrical about their Irish family tree and their long, ancient line of ancestors somewhere back in Ireland.

In fact, more than 30 million of us (for perspective, that's almost six times the population of the Republic of Ireland!) now claim to have Irish roots, with most of those today living in New England.

But in their everyday lives, many of these people will seem as American as apple pie, not as Irish as a pint of Guinness! Understandably, thanks to the passage of time, as the number of generations between us and our Irish lineage has increased, our claim to Irish heritage can sometimes seem a little tenuous. (New England, after all, is more than 2,500 miles away from the Emerald Isle!)

So, how much do you *really* know about Ireland, Irish history, and Irish culture? That is precisely what this book is here to find out...

This is the *Ultimate Irish Challenge*, a unique collection of Irish trivia questions—covering everything from Ireland's geography and music to great Irish writers, movie stars, sports stars, rock and pop stars, and much, much more.

There are questions here on Ireland's counties and cities, major cultural figures, poets, authors, and history. There are even questions dedicated to Irish folklore that will test your knowledge of Ireland's centuries-old myths and legends, as well as questions dedicated to its politics and modern history, bringing your knowledge right up to date with modern Ireland in the 21st century.

There are 15 chapters of questions in this book, each dedicated to a different aspect of Irish culture, history, and life. In total, there are more than 200 multiple-choice and true-or-false trivia questions for you to tackle, all specially compiled to test your Irishness to its limits!

Don't worry if one or more of these questions stump you, of course. The full solutions to each quiz (along with some further context and explanations, wherever necessary) are included after each chapter. And along the way, keep your eyes peeled for lots of interesting trivia and delightful did-you-knows, perfect for proudly dropping into your next conversation about your Irish heritage!

So, let's get started, shall we? Pour yourself a nice tall glass of Irish stout (in which case, *slainte!*) or else brew up a delicious Irish breakfast tea (if that's more your thing), and let's get this test of your general knowledge of Ireland underway…

CHAPTER 1
IRISH GENERAL KNOWLEDGE

We're going to start things off easily here, with a quick pot-luck quiz on all things Irish. The questions in this first chapter cover different subjects, but they are all rather simple—so you can think of this first set of questions as something of a warm-up for what is to come!

1. The stripes on the flag of the Republic of Ireland are green, white, and what other color?

    a. Yellow

    b. Red

    c. Orange

    d. Blue

2. Who is the patron saint of Ireland…

    a. St. George

    b. St. Andrew

    c. St. Thomas

    d. St. Patrick

3. …and the patron saint of Ireland is popularly said to have rid the island of what creatures?

    a. Snakes

    b. Birds

    c. Spiders

    d. Bears

4. Which famous Irish poet's first and middle names were William and Butler?

    a. Moore

    b. Yeats

    c. Heaney

    d. Tynan

5. Dublin lies on which of Ireland's coasts?

    a. North

    b. South

    c. East

    d. West

6. What musical instrument is considered one of the national symbols of Ireland?

    a. Violin

    b. Flute

    c. Harp

    d. Trumpet

7. Who is the lead singer of the Irish rock band U2?

    a. Robert Smith

    b. Bono

    c. Michael Stipe

    d. Ray Davies

8. *Éire* is the Irish name for…what?

    a. England

    b. Ireland

    c. Europe

    d. America

9. True or False. The Irish city of Waterford is well known for its fine ironware.

    a. True

    b. False

10. In what century did Ireland experience a devastating four-year famine?

a. 9th century

b. 14th century

c. 17th century

d. 19th century

11. Which of these famous writers was NOT born in Ireland?

a. Bram Stoker

b. George Bernard Shaw

c. JRR Tolkien

d. Oscar Wilde

12. The shamrock, a popular symbol of Ireland, is a type of what plant?

a. Clover

b. Primrose

c. Daffodil

d. Daisy

13. In Ireland, what is *Aer Lingus*?

a. The Irish language

b. The national anthem

c. An airline

d. The police service

14. The Irish town of Cobh, formerly Queenstown, has a famous connection to…what?

a. Elvis Presley

b. The RMS *Titanic*

c. The Statue of Liberty

d. John F. Kennedy

SOLUTIONS

1. C. Orange. The colors on the Irish flag are meant to represent a truce (white) between Ireland's Catholic (green) and Protestant (orange) populations. Although the design of the flag itself dates back to the mid-1800s, it has only been considered the official flag of the Irish Republic since 1922.
2. D. St. Patrick. The feast day of St. Patrick is famously celebrated on March 17.
3. A. Snakes. Despite the popularity of the story, however, archeological evidence suggests that snakes have not been present in Ireland since at least the end of the last Ice Age— so there were none for St. Patrick to banish in the first place!
4. B. Yeats. WB Yeats rejected many of his contemporaries' love of modernist free verse and wrote some of Ireland's most beautiful lyrical and traditional poetry in the early 1900s. He was awarded the Nobel Prize for Literature in 1923.
5. C. East. Dublin stands on Ireland's east coast, making it the largest port on the Irish Sea.
6. C. Harp. The *cláirseach*, or Celtic harp, holds such an important position in Irish culture that an image of a golden harp appears on the Irish coat of arms.
7. B. Bono. Born in Dublin in 1960, Bono's real name is Paul David Hewson.
8. B. Ireland. The name *Éire* is thought to derive from the name of an ancient Gaelic goddess, Eriu, who came to symbolize the Irish world.
9. False. Waterford is actually celebrated for its local glassware, known as Waterford Crystal.

10. C. 19th century. Ireland's so-called Great Famine lasted for four years, from 1845 to 1849, during which time more than one million people starved and another one-and-a-half million emigrated. The famine was so devastating that the country's population has never recovered; once, more than eight million people called Ireland home, but even in the 2020s, the population of the entire island—north and south of the border—is just over 7.5 million.

11. C. JRR Tolkien. *Lord of the Rings* author Tolkien was actually born in Bloemfontein, in what is now modern-day South Africa, in 1892.

12. A. Clover. Although the name is sometimes wrongly associated with the supposedly lucky "four-leaf" clover, a shamrock actually has three leaves. This is seen by many to be a religious symbol representing God, Jesus, and the Holy Spirit.

13. C. An airline. Aer Lingus is actually the flag-carrying national airline of Ireland, founded by the Irish government in 1936.

14. B. The RMS *Titanic*. On April 11, 1912, Cobh—which was at the time known as Queenstown—was the final port of call of the RMS *Titanic* before she set out across the Atlantic on her ill-fated maiden voyage.

DID YOU KNOW?

Despite his attachment to Ireland, St. Patrick is actually believed to have been born in England sometime around the 5th century.

HOW BONO GOT HIS NAME

He might be known to legions of music fans around the world as Bono, but in his teens, U2 frontman Paul Hewson tried out several nicknames before he and the rest of the band came together in the mid-1970s.

In his teens, Hewson was part of an experimental surrealist gang of musicians and artists, many of whom likewise went by aliases and nicknames. Initially, the artist we now know as Bono went by the fairly unwieldy moniker of "Steinhegvanhuysenolegbangbangbang" — or just "Huysemann" for short! Thankfully, the gang saw fit to change Hewson's name and eventually settled on Bono (or rather, "Bono Vox," as he was originally known in full). The name might have caught on, but it had an unusual inspiration: "Bonavox" was the name of a store in the center of the city of Dublin selling hearing aids and other apparatus for the deaf and hearing impaired.

It wasn't only Bono who struggled to find a name that would stand the test of time, either — when he left his gang behind and formed a band, the group we now know as U2 started gigging in and around Dublin under the name Feedback in 1976. The following year, they changed their name to The Hype, before a second change of heart saw them adopt the name U2 in 1978.

CHAPTER 2
GEOGRAPHY

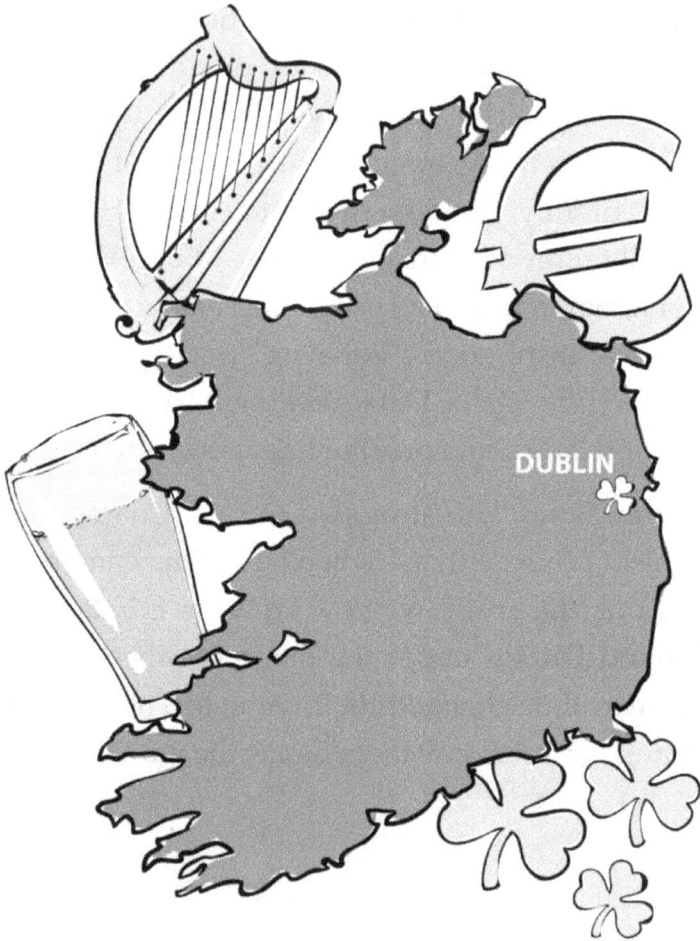

At just over 32,000 square miles, the island of Ireland is the third largest in Europe and one of the largest islands in the world—larger even than Hokkaido in Japan and Hispaniola in the Caribbean. Partitioned between the North and South (with Northern Ireland constituting part of the United Kingdom and the southern Republic of Ireland remaining an independent nation), Ireland is known for its rugged coasts and mountains. It has vast expanses of lush green open land—the greenness of which is what gives the island its nickname, The Emerald Isle!

This next set of questions celebrates this beautiful and unique place's extraordinary landscape and quizzes your knowledge of Ireland's rivers and seas, hills and mountains, towns, cities, counties, and provinces.

1. What is the Republic of Ireland's northernmost county, which shares the vast majority of its border with Northern Ireland?

    a. Leitrim
    b. Laois
    c. Wexford
    d. Donegal

2. What is Ireland's longest river?

    a. Slaney
    b. Barrow
    c. Liffey
    d. Shannon

3. Ireland has four provinces. Which of these is NOT one of them?

a. Ulster

b. Leinster

c. Munster

d. Leitrim

4. Located in County Tipperary, what are the Silvermines in the center of Ireland?

    a. Valleys

    b. Mountains

    c. Lakes

    d. Caves

5. The North Channel separates the island of Ireland from which other country?

    a. France

    b. Wales

    c. England

    d. Scotland

6. The Republic of Ireland takes up how much of the island of Ireland?

    a. 40%

    b. 55%

    c. 70%

    d. 85%

7. Almost one-quarter of the entire Irish population—1.2 million people—live in Dublin. But with a population of just over 220,000, what is the Republic of Ireland's second-largest city?

    a. Wexford

    b. Cork

    c. Tipperary

    d. Limerick

8. Which of these Irish counties is located furthest south?

    a. Galway

    b. Kerry

    c. Louth

    d. Cavan

9. Ireland has three counties whose names begin with the letter M. Name one of them.

    _____

10. What is the name of the body of water that lies off the south coast of Ireland?

    a. Norwegian Sea

    b. North Sea

    c. Celtic Sea

    d. North Channel

11. Ireland's highest mountain, Carrauntoohil, is located in a range of mountains called…what?

    a. MacGillycuddy's Reeks

    b. MacMasterson's Hums

    c. MacAloon's Stench

    d. MacFlanaghoon's Stinks

12. In what Irish county are the famous sea cliffs of Moher?

    a. Clare

    b. Kerry

    c. Cork

    d. Carlow

13. Ireland's famous Aran Islands archipelago stands in what body of water?

    a. Lough Neagh

    b. Galway Bay

    c. Irish Sea

    d. Bristol Channel

14. Which of these Irish port cities is a major ferry terminal connected by sea to locations across the UK and Europe?

    a. Ardmore

    b. Drogheda

    c. Bray

    d. Rosslare

SOLUTIONS

1. D. Donegal. In fact, County Donegal shares such a long border with Northern Ireland that only 7% of its land border is shared with the rest of the Irish Republic.
2. D. Shannon. The River Shannon flows south through much of central Ireland, covering 220 miles in total.
3. D. Leitrim. The fourth province is Connacht, in northwestern Ireland.
4. B. Mountains. Despite their name, the Silvermine Mountains rise above the land, not below it, reaching a height of over 2,000 ft.
5. D. Scotland. The sea strait between the island of Ireland and Scotland, known as the Sea of Moyle, is the narrowest water passage between Ireland and Great Britain. Despite being just 12 miles wide at its narrowest point, the Sea of Moyle is also the deepest of all the seas in the British Isles, reaching a depth of 1,024 ft at a spot known as Beaufort's Dyke.
6. D. 85%. The remaining 15% of the island of Ireland forms Northern Ireland, which is part of the United Kingdom.
7. B. Cork. Cork takes its name from an Irish word, *corach*, meaning "marshland."
8. B. Kerry. Both County Cavan and County Louth are among Ireland's northernmost counties and share their border with Northern Ireland. County Galway is located on Ireland's west coast, roughly due west of Dublin, while County Kerry occupies the far southwest corner of Ireland; only County Cork extends any further south.

9. Mayo, Meath, or Monaghan. Each one is in a different Irish province: Mayo is in Connacht, Meath is in Leinster, and Monaghan is in Ulster.

10. C. Celtic Sea. The Celtic Sea stretches from southern Ireland across to Wales and southwest England, and it is bordered at its furthest south by France's Bay of Biscay.

11. A. MacGillycuddy's Reeks. The "reek" in the name of this mountain range has nothing to do with foul smells but comes from an Irish word, *cruach*, for a mound or peak. The highest mountain in the Reeks, Carrauntoohil, stands over 3,400 ft tall.

12. C. Clare. The enormous Cliffs of Moher are one of Ireland's most popular tourist attractions, rising to a height of over 700 ft on the island's far west coast.

13. B. Galway Bay. The three Aran Islands of Inishmore, Inishmaan, and Inisheer lie across the mouth of Galway Bay. Incredibly, they have been inhabited for more than 3,000 years. Despite their relative remoteness, today they are still home to more than 1,000 people.

14. D. Rosslare. The ferry port at Rosslare is connected to locations as far afield as Bilbao, Santander, and Cherbourg.

DID YOU KNOW?

At 224 miles long, Ireland's River Shannon is so vast that its waters drain a basin covering almost a quarter of the entire island!

THE MEN WHO (UNKNOWINGLY) OWNED IRELAND'S HIGHEST MOUNTAIN

For many years, walkers and climbers have wandered freely in the Reeks mountains of central Ireland, climbing Ireland's highest peak, Carrauntoohil, without thought. In 2006, however, research by a climber and author named Jim Ryan discovered that the land on which Carrauntoohil stands—and indeed the mountain itself—is privately owned.

The great-grandfathers of four local landowners and farmers purchased the freehold for the mountain from the Irish Land Commission in the 19th century. They had been paying a fee of 11 shillings and two pence (equivalent to around 80 US cents) twice a year for decades. All the walkers and climbers of Carrauntoohil were essentially trespassing on the four farmers' land and could be ejected at any time if the farmers wished to exercise their legal ownership.

The discovery has led to considerable debate in Ireland over whether such longstanding agreements—which would understandably never be granted today!—should be upheld, or whether the Irish government should exercise its power to force purchase of the land. In doing so, they would remove all ownership rights to Ireland's highest mountain and its surrounding peaks. This would, in effect, convert the entire area into a national park, securing the Irish people's freedom to walk and climb there in the future.

As of the 2020s, however, no such forcible purchase order has ever been made, and so strictly speaking, Carrauntoohil and its surrounding mountains remain under private leasehold. In his book, Jim Ryan rightly commended the landowners for allowing visitors to walk and climb the area free of charge — despite the risk of damage to their property and farmland!

CHAPTER 3

IRELAND IN THE MOVIES I

For an island with a relatively small population, Ireland has a remarkably successful and impactful cinematic record, including dozens of Oscar winners and a long line of successful movies.

This chapter of questions is the first of two celebrating Irish cinema and Ireland's impact on Hollywood—from classic movie greats to modern blockbusters and Oscar-nominated icons.

1. Which Irish actor won an Oscar in 2024 for his performance in the Christopher Nolan biopic *Oppenheimer*?

    a. Colin Farrell
    b. Cillian Murphy
    c. Colm Meaney
    d. Brendan Gleeson

2. What was the first movie in which Irish superstar Pierce Brosnan played James Bond?

    a. *Tomorrow Never Dies*
    b. *Die Another Day*
    c. *Goldeneye*
    d. *The World Is Not Enough*

3. Acclaimed Irish actress Brenda Fricker won an Oscar for her performance opposite Daniel Day-Lewis in *My Left Foot*—but to millions of movie fans, she's best known for a memorable supporting role in what children's movie sequel?

    a. *The Addams Family Values*
    b. *Home Alone 2: Lost in New York*
    c. *Spy Kids 2*
    d. *Paddington 2*

4. Which legendary actor and knight of the realm was born in Belfast in 1960 and, in 2022, won an Oscar for the screenplay to his semi-autobiographical retelling of his childhood, also called *Belfast*?

    a. Sir Ian McKellen
    b. Sir Patrick Stewart
    c. Sir Kenneth Branagh
    d. Sir Ben Kingsley

5. Who starred opposite Maureen O'Hara in the 1952 movie *The Quiet Man*, which was one of the first Hollywood movies in which the Irish language was heard on screen?

    a. Clint Eastwood
    b. John Wayne
    c. James Stewart
    d. Clark Gable

6. Which British actress starred opposite Daniel Day-Lewis in the critically acclaimed 1993 drama *In the Name of the Father*?

    a. Kate Beckinsale
    b. Emma Thompson
    c. Helena Bonham Carter
    d. Tilda Swinton

7. Which Irish actor connects the Hollywood movies *300*, *Inglourious Basterds*, *X-Men: First Class*, and *Prometheus*?

    a. Cillian Murphy
    b. Ciarán Hinds
    c. Michael Fassbender
    d. Aidan Turner

8. In what 2018 horror movie did Irish actor Gabriel Byrne star together with Toni Collette as a haunted family struggling to come to terms with the loss of their daughter?

    a. *Malignant*
    b. *Insidious*
    c. *St. Maud*
    d. *Hereditary*

9. For her role in what 2007 period drama was Irish actress Saoirse Ronan nominated for the Academy Award for Best Supporting Actress at the age of just 13?

    a. *Pride and Prejudice*
    b. *The Duchess*
    c. *Atonement*
    d. *Young Victoria*

10. Who did Irish actor Johnathan Rhys Meyers play in the acclaimed television serial *The Tudors*?

    a. Henry VIII
    b. Sir Walter Raleigh
    c. Prince Edward
    d. Thomas Cromwell

11. Which legendary half-Irish actor was nominated for the Academy Award for Best Actor on eight separate occasions but never won a competitive Oscar in a career spanning six decades?

    a. Peter O'Toole
    b. Dudley Moore
    c. Michael Gambon
    d. Richard Harris

12. Which Irish actress of stage and screen—who was nominated for Primetime Emmy Awards for her roles in *Fleabag* and *Killing Eve*—played Harry Potter's aunt, Petunia, in the long-running *Harry Potter* movie series?

    a. Nicola Coughlan
    b. Fionn O'Shea
    c. Olwen Fouéré
    d. Fiona Shaw

13. What kind of being did Irish actors Aidan Turner and James Nesbitt play in Peter Jackson's *The Hobbit* trilogy?

    a. Hobbits
    b. Dragons
    c. Dwarves
    d. Elves

14. Which Irish actor played a manipulative Oxford University student who takes advantage of a monied family in the 2023 dark comedy-drama *Saltburn*?

    a. Colin Farrell
    b. Domhnall Gleeson
    c. Daryl McCormack
    d. Barry Keoghan

SOLUTIONS

1. B. Cillian Murphy. Murphy's Best Actor Academy Award was one of seven the movie took home on Oscar night, including Best Picture, Best Director for Christopher Nolan, and Best Supporting Actor for Robert Downey, Jr.

2. C. *Goldeneye*. Brosnan played James Bond in all four of these movies, of which the first was *Goldeneye*, released in 1997. His last role as Bond was in 2002's *Die Another Day* before the role was handed over to Daniel Craig for 2006's *Casino Royale*.

3. B. *Home Alone 2: Lost in New York*. Fricker played the unnamed Pigeon Lady in 1992's sequel to *Home Alone*.

4. C. Sir Kenneth Branagh. *Belfast* was nominated for a total of seven Oscars at the 94th Academy Awards in 2022, including supporting performance nominations for Dame Judi Dench and Ciarán Hinds.

5. B. John Wayne. Directed by John Ford, *The Quiet Man* was one of the year's most successful movies, grossing almost $4 million at the 1952 box office and earning Ford his fourth Academy Award for Best Director.

6. B. Emma Thompson. Both Thompson and Day-Lewis were nominated for Oscars for their performances in *In the Name of the Father*, which retold the true-life story of four men wrongly convicted of an Irish terrorist attack in Guildford, Surrey, in 1974.

7. C. Michael Fassbender. Born in Germany in 1977, Michael Fassbender's mother was from Northern Ireland, and the

family relocated to Killarney, in County Kerry, when he was two years old.

8. D. *Hereditary*. The movie was one of the most highly acclaimed of the year and, despite a limited release, grossed almost $100 million at the box office, becoming the most successful movie to date for independent production company A24.

9. C. *Atonement*. Adapted from the 2001 novel by Ian McEwan, *Atonement* told the story of the repercussions of a crime played out over six decades. Ronan played one of the lead characters, an aspiring novelist, at her youngest in the story and won universal acclaim for her performance.

10. A. Henry VIII. The four seasons of *The Tudors* charted almost the entirety of Henry VIII's reign, including his six marriages. Its all-star cast included future *Superman* star Henry Cavill as the Duke of Suffolk and Sam Neill as Cardinal Wolsey.

11. A. Peter O'Toole. Incredibly, Peter O'Toole's eight nominated roles span more than 40 years of his career, beginning with *Lawrence of Arabia* in 1962 and ending with the comedy-drama *Venus* in 2006. Although he never won the Academy Award competitively, in 2002 he was honored with an Honorary Award recognizing his lifelong contribution to the world of cinema.

12. D. Fiona Shaw. Shaw is also known for her roles in the sci-fi series *Andor* and *True Detective: Night Country*.

13. C. Dwarves. Nesbitt played Bofur in *The Hobbit* trilogy, while Turner played Kíli—two members of the company of dwarves who seek to regain control of the Misty Mountain from the dragon Smaug.

14. D. Barry Keoghan. Keoghan was nominated for a BAFTA for his role in *Saltburn* alongside costars Jacob Elordi and Rosamund Pike.

DID YOU KNOW?

The full list of Irish Oscar nominees in cinema history includes one very surprising name: the playwright George Bernard Shaw won the 1938 Academy Award for Best Screenplay for his adaptation of his own play Pygmalion!

THE IRISHMAN WHO MADE OSCAR HISTORY

If you were to name a legendary Hollywood actor from Ireland, chances are today you might pick someone along the lines of Liam Neeson, Colin Farrell, or Pierce Brosnan. Oscar-winner Barry Fitzgerald might not be top of anyone's list today, it's fair to say, but this icon of Hollywood's Golden Age holds an utterly unique place in both Hollywood's and the Academy Awards' history.

Fitzgerald had already appeared in movies such as *Bringing Up Baby* (1938), *The Long Voyage Home* (1940), and *How Green Was My Valley* (1941) when he was cast opposite Bing Crosby in the 1944 musical comedy-drama *Going My Way*. Considered by many as

Fitzgerald's breakthrough role, the movie was a box office smash and was nominated for ten Oscars at the 17th Academy Awards the following year, winning a total of seven (including Best Picture, Best Actor for Bing Crosby, and Best Original Song for the classic track "Swinging on a Star").

Fitzgerald also took home an Oscar that night, winning the Academy Award for Best Supporting Actor for his role as Father Fitzgibbon in the movie (and seeing off stiff competition from the likes of Claude Rains and Clifton Webb). But oddly, Fitzgerald's performance in the movie was seemingly so memorable that he found himself in the odd position of being simultaneously nominated against his costar, Bing Crosby, in the Best Actor category too. Crosby may have beat him to the lead actor award, but there was at one point the potential, at least, for Fitzgerald to take home two Oscars for the same role!

Needless to say, this bizarre dual nomination has never occurred again: after Fitzgerald found himself put forward for an award in two categories for the same role in the same movie, the Academy quickly changed its rules the following year to prevent such a situation from ever arising again!

CHAPTER 4
IRISH MUSIC I

From U2 to Enya and from Van Morrison to the Pogues, Irish pop and rock acts routinely rank among the world's most popular, successful, and best-selling. But the story of Irish music is not only concerned with modern pop and rock, as the long tradition of Irish folk tunes and melodies — many dating back several centuries! — will easily attest.

This is the first of two chapters celebrating all aspects of Irish music, from traditional folk songs and local acts to modern pop and rock, and some of the best-selling artists in the musical world today.

1. The Irish national anthem is called *Amhrán na bhFiann*. What does that title translate to in English?

    a. *The Lover's Song*
    b. *The Actor's Song*
    c. *The Soldier's Song*
    d. *The Dancer's Song*

2. The Irish music superstar Enya was nominated for an Academy Award for Best Original Song for her track "May It Be." In what hugely successful movie series was it used?

    a. *Harry Potter*
    b. *The Lord of the Rings*
    c. *James Bond*
    d. *The Hunger Games*

3. Which legendary Irish artist had a Billboard Top 10 hit in 1967 with the track "Brown Eyed Girl"?

    a. The Pogues
    b. Thin Lizzy

    c. Van Morrison

    d. Rory Gallagher

4. Which Irish folk-pop act consists of the four siblings Andrea, Caroline, Sharon, and Jim?

    a. Clannad

    b. The Dubliners

    c. The Chieftains

    d. The Corrs

5. What 1987 album by Irish rock band U2 featured the tracks "With or Without You," "I Still Haven't Found What I'm Looking For," and "Where the Streets Have No Name"?

    a. *War*

    b. *All That You Can't Leave Behind*

    c. *The Joshua Tree*

    d. *Rattle and Hum*

6. Phil Lynott is the lead singer and frontman of what legendary Irish rock band?

    a. The Cranberries

    b. Thin Lizzy

    c. The Undertones

    d. The Boomtown Rays

7. What classic 1979 single by an Irish pop act opens with the line, "The silicon chip inside her head / Gets switched to overload"?

    a. "Zombie"

    b. "Teenage Kicks"

    c. "Dirty Old Town"

    d. "I Don't Like Mondays"

8. In what year did Irish rockstar Hozier have a worldwide hit with the track "Take Me to Church"?

   a. 2003
   b. 2008
   c. 2013
   d. 2018

9. What classic Irish folk tune opens with the line, "In the year of our Lord 1806 / We set sail from the fair quay of Cork"?

   a. "The Irish Rover"
   b. "The Parting Glass"
   c. "I Know My Love"
   d. "The Sea Around Us"

10. Sinéad O'Connor had a global smash hit in 1990 with the song "Nothing Compares 2 U" — but who wrote it?

   a. Sting
   b. Bruce Springsteen
   c. Prince
   d. Quincy Jones

11. In what year did Irish superstar Gilbert O'Sullivan have a Number 1 hit on the Billboard Charts with "Alone Again (Naturally)"?

   a. 1969
   b. 1972
   c. 1976
   d. 1979

12. According to the lyrics of the Irish folk tune of the same name, what is the name of the beautiful young woman known as "the Rose of Tralee"?

a. Morag

b. Molly

c. Mary

d. Maureen

13. By what nickname is U2's lead guitarist David Howell Evans better known?

a. The Edge

b. The Side

c. The Border

d. The Threshold

14. The lyrics to the famous Irish folksong "Danny Boy" were actually written by an Englishman, who never set foot in Ireland. True or False?

a. True

b. False

SOLUTIONS

1. C. "The Soldier's Song." "The Soldier's Song" was written sometime around 1910. The lyrics—which were originally written in English before being translated into Irish in 1923—were written by republican composer Peadar Kearney, while his childhood friend (and next-door neighbor) Patrick Heeney penned the music. Although the full song has three fairly lengthy verses, only the chorus is typically used as the Irish anthem.

2. B. *The Lord of the Rings*. Enya provided two original songs to Peter Jackson's *Lord of the Rings* trilogy, with the track "May It Be" earning her Oscar, Golden Globe, and Grammy nominations.

3. C. Van Morrison. "Brown Eyed Girl" was Northern Ireland–born superstar Van Morrison's debut single and his first Billboard Top 10 Hit. He reached his highest position on the Billboard chart two years later when his track "Domino" reached Number 9 in 1970.

4. D. The Corrs. The Corrs reached their highest position on the Billboard chart in 2001 with their global smash hit "Breathless."

5. C. *The Joshua Tree*. *The Joshua Tree* remains one of U2's most successful and highly acclaimed albums, selling more than ten million copies in the US alone and seeing off competition from the likes of Michael Jackson's *Bad* and Prince's *Sign of the Times* to win the 1988 Grammy Award for Album of the Year.

6. B. Thin Lizzy. Formed in Dublin in 1969, Thin Lizzy is best known for classic 1970s hits like "Whiskey in the Jar" and "The Boys Are Back in Town."

7. D. "I Don't Like Mondays." Although the song only reached a relatively lowly Number 73 in the US, The Boomtown Rats' "I Don't Like Mondays" was a smash hit around the world and remains one of the band's most popular and best-known tracks.

8. C. 2013. The song peaked at Number 2 on the Billboard Hot 100 and has been certified 13 x Platinum in the US alone!

9. A. "The Irish Rover." The track became a worldwide hit in 1987 when it was covered by Irish groups The Pogues and The Dubliners.

10. C. Prince. The pair had not properly met prior to O'Connor covering Prince's track in 1990, but according to Sinéad O'Connor's memoir, *Rememberings*, when they did eventually meet, they did not get along—and ended up having a pillow fight!

11. B. 1972. The track ended up spending six non-consecutive weeks at the top of the Billboard charts across the summer and autumn of 1972. It also reached Number 1 in Canada.

12. C. Mary. As the song explains, "She was lovely and fair as the rose of the summer, / Yet 'twas not her beauty alone that won me, / Oh no, 'twas the truth in her eyes ever dawning, / That made me love Mary, the Rose of Tralee."

13. A. The Edge. No one has ever definitively explained the origin of Evans' nickname, though a popular fan theory claims it refers to the rather pointed shape of his head!

14. True! The lyrics are the work of an Oxford-educated English lawyer named Frederic Weatherly, who wrote them in 1910.

They were first set to music three years later when they were adapted to fit an old Irish folk tune called the "Londonderry Air." (Turn the page for a little more on the history of "Danny Boy"!)

DID YOU KNOW?

Although rock acts like U2, Thin Lizzy, Snow Patrol, and The Script rank among Ireland's most successful music groups, the best-selling solo artist in Irish musical history is Enya — who, despite never touring, has sold more than 80 million records worldwide!

THE MAN WHO MADE NOTHING FROM DANNY BOY

As we have just seen, despite its popularity in Ireland—and with singers around the world for that matter—the song "Danny Boy" has a rather bizarre history, thanks to its somewhat distant lyricist, Frederic Weatherly.

It remains unclear whose idea it was to take Weatherly's lyrics and set them to the famous "Londonderry Air," with various composers taking credit (or being credited) over the years. According to one tale, however, Weatherly originally had another tune in mind for his lyrics until his sister-in-law, Margaret "Jess" Enright, sent him the tune to "Londonderry Air" and suggested he use that instead. The pairing of Weatherly's lyrics and the stately tune Enright had proposed worked brilliantly, and the song became an immense success. It has since been recorded by countless artists all over the world, ranging from Irish superstar Sinéad O'Connor to rather more unlikely names such as Harry Belafonte, Paul Robeson, and Patti LaBelle.

The success of the song understandably made it a major money-spinner for Weatherly—but according to reports, he never once acknowledged his sister-in-law's input into his and the song's success. Claiming instead that the track was entirely his own idea, Weatherly's obstinacy allegedly caused a deep rift in his family that drove him and his brother, Edward, apart. While Weatherly continued to reap the rewards of the song's success, Edward and Jess saw nothing of its popularity and would go on to die in poverty.

CHAPTER 5

IRISH HISTORY I

The history of Ireland stretches back many thousands of years, and over the centuries, the island has been settled and colonized by countless groups, from the Romans and the Normans to the Celts and the English.

This chapter is the first of two that will test your knowledge of all aspects of Irish history, both ancient and modern.

1. By what name did the Romans know the island of Ireland?

    a. Britannia
    b. Caledonia
    c. Hibernia
    d. Cambria

2. In ancient Ireland, what was *ogham*?

    a. A drink
    b. A method of writing
    c. A lamb stew
    d. A folk dance

3. James Hoban was born in Callan, in Ireland's County Kilkenny, in 1755. Americans will know him as the designer of…what?

    a. The White House
    b. The Statue of Liberty
    c. The dollar bill
    d. The Stars and Stripes

4. Which US president was involved in the signing of the Good Friday Agreement, which famously ended The Troubles in Northern Ireland?

    a. Dwight D. Eisenhower
    b. Richard Nixon

c. Bill Clinton

d. Barrack Obama

5. Seen as a major step forward in ending British rule in Ireland, in what year did the infamous Easter Rising take place?

    a. 1886

    b. 1896

    c. 1906

    d. 1916

6. Who first invaded Ireland in the late 8th century and remained there, exercising ever greater control, for at least the next 300 years?

    a. The Normans

    b. The Vikings

    c. The Angles

    d. The Visigoths

7. In what decade was the Republic of Ireland officially declared, and Ireland officially withdrew from the British Commonwealth?

    a. 1920s

    b. 1940s

    c. 1960s

    d. 1980s

8. The Williamite War was a bitter conflict fought in Ireland from 1689 to 1691, between the largely Protestant supporters of King William III and the largely Catholic supporters of which other monarch, whom William had recently replaced on the British throne?

a. Elizabeth I
b. George III
c. James II
d. Charles II

9. Which infamous figure from British history sacked the Irish city of Drogheda in 1649?

a. Oliver Cromwell
b. Francis Drake
c. Walter Raleigh
d. Henry VIII

10. In the early 17th century, thousands of people from Scotland and northern England were actively encouraged to move to Northern Ireland, where they were granted swaths of arable land that had been confiscated from native Irish Gaelic chiefs by the English crown. Under what name did this enforced land grab later become known?

a. The Plantation of Ulster
b. The Colonization of Munster
c. The Occupation of Connacht
d. The Settlement of Leinster

11. Despite it being a predominantly Catholic country, no Irish-born person has ever been elected Pope. True or False?

a. True
b. False

12. One of the most important military engagements in Irish history was the Battle of the Boyne. But what is the Boyne?

a. A monastery
b. A castle

c. A mountain

d. A river

13. The patroness saint of Ireland, St. Brigid, is particularly associated with which Irish town?

    a. Kildare

    b. Ennis

    c. Navan

    d. Clonmel

14. In 2019, the Irish people voted in a referendum — by a margin of 82% to 18% — to amend the former rules surrounding the legality of what in Ireland?

    a. Divorce

    b. Adoption

    c. Suffrage

    d. Cohabitation

SOLUTIONS

1. C. Hibernia. Caledonia was the Roman name for Scotland, Britannia was Britain, and Cambria was Wales. The name Hibernia itself is popularly said to mean "land of winters," in reference to Ireland's famously intemperate weather!

2. B. A method of writing. Dating back more than 1,600 years, the Ogham script was written as a series of straight and diagonal strokes on either side of a central linking line known as the stem. Many of the script's 20 letters were named after trees, including *dair* ("oak"), *coll* ("hazel"), and *fearn* ("alder").

3. A. The White House. Hoban emigrated to the United States after the Revolutionary War and, in 1785, established himself as an architect in Philadelphia. In 1792, he entered a competition—overseen by George Washington and Thomas Jefferson—to design the presidential residence at the center of the newly established federal city of Washington, DC. Of the nine entrants, it was his design that was chosen.

4. C. Bill Clinton. During a period of ceasefire during The Troubles in 1995, Bill Clinton became the first president in US history to visit Northern Ireland and used his official visit to Belfast to urge the peace talks that would eventually end the conflict. Three long years of lengthy discussions between warring factions across the Northern and Southern Irish border followed before the Good Friday peace agreement was finally ratified in 1998.

5. D. 1916. Home rule in Ireland had already been enacted by parliament in 1914, but the outbreak of World War I led to it

being suspended. The Easter Rising of 1916—an armed Irish Republican protest against Britain's rule of Ireland during Easter Week of that year—put home rule back on the table. Britain's brutal execution of the Irish protestors who had carried out the uprising only served to enflame Irish interest in ending British rule once and for all, and ultimately Ireland became independent in 1922.

6. B. The Vikings. An unidentified island recorded only as *"Rechru"* was the first Irish territory attacked by the Vikings in 795 CE. Over the years that followed, Scandinavian settlements were established all across Ireland, including in the cities of Dublin, Limerick, and Waterford.

7. B. 1940s. The Republic of Ireland was officially declared in 1949; before then, Ireland had been the Irish Free State and had operated as a constitutional monarchy with the king as its official head of state. Ireland's declaration as a republic, removing the king as its figurehead, was in contravention of the British Commonwealth's rules, and Ireland left the Commonwealth as a result. Ironically, the rules disallowing republics from being members of the Commonwealth were changed just ten days later, but Ireland did not reapply for membership and has not been a Commonwealth nation ever since.

8. C. James II. The so-called Glorious Revolution had seen the Catholic King James lose his hold on the British throne, replaced by his Protestant daughter Mary II and her husband William III. James still retained a lot of support among the Catholic "Jacobites" of Ireland, however, leading to a bloody conflict between the two kings' supporters there. The war proved a bitter defeat for King James, and the

victory of the Protestants led to further suppression of Catholicism across Britain and Ireland.

9. A. Oliver Cromwell. After Cromwell's parliamentarians oversaw the execution of Charles I and installed his Commonwealth of England in place of the royal family, Ireland—which was at that time under England's rule—responded in uproar, and royalist protests broke out across the island. Cromwell countered with bloodthirsty violence, arriving at the port of Drogheda, just north of Dublin, in 1649 and there massacring more than 3,000 royalist supporters.

10. A. The Plantation of Ulster. More than half a million acres (1,200 square miles) of farmland changed hands during the Plantation era, which is seen by many as the first step on the road to the later partition of Northern and Southern Ireland.

11. True! In fact, there have only been 17 Irish cardinals in the entire history of the Catholic Church, with the first—Paul Cullen, the former Metropolitan Archbishop of Dublin—elected in 1866.

12. D. A river. The Battle of the Boyne, in 1690, was one of the major clashes of Ireland's Williamite Wars. It was fought across the banks of the river Boyne, which flows for around 70 miles across northeast Ireland, emptying into the Irish Sea close to the town of Drogheda.

13. A. Kildare. St. Brigid of Kildare, as she is also known, is said to have founded Kildare Abbey in the 5th century.

14. A. Divorce. The referendum saw the enactment of the 38th Amendment of the Irish Constitution, which removed a longstanding requirement that couples wishing to divorce observe a period of separation before initiating legal proceedings.

DID YOU KNOW?

The discovery of a carved reindeer bone in an isolated cave in County Cork in 2021 suggests that humans have been living in Ireland far longer than previously thought. Incredibly, the discovery suggests Ireland may have been inhabited for more than 33,000 years!

HOW ST. VALENTINE ENDED UP IN DUBLIN

A number of saints are venerated in Ireland, but perhaps the most surprising is one that has little to no historical connection to the island at all: St. Valentine.

Despite his association with a rather commercialized holiday today, St. Valentine was a real historical figure and a martyred saint of ancient Europe. Born in the Italian city of Terni (now in Umbria, but at that time part of the Roman province of Italia) in the early 3rd century CE, Valentine first became a priest before being elevated to the position of Bishop of Terni during the city's Roman control. In that role, he began ministering to imprisoned and persecuted Christians. This understandably led to Valentine falling foul of the Roman Empire, and he was called before Emperor Claudius II.

Although the emperor initially warmed to the kindly and pious Bishop Valentine (or Valentinus, as he was known to the Latin-speaking Romans), that changed when Valentine tried to convince the emperor to convert to Christianity. Instead, Claudius turned Valentine's offer around: he demanded Valentine renounce his Christian faith and embrace the Roman religion or else be executed. Valentine refused and so was beaten and beheaded outside of Rome's famous Flaminian Gate on February 14 — the feast day of St. Valentine — in 269 CE.

Almost 1,600 years later, an Irish Carmelite monk named John Spratt was visiting Rome, around the time that a relic belonging to an ancient church dedicated to St. Valentine was discovered. While in Rome, Spratt's work as a Jesuit preacher brought him to the attention of the Vatican, and to Pope Gregory XVI himself. The pope decided to reward Spratt's ministering with a gift and so sent some of the recently discovered remains of St. Valentine from Rome to Dublin.

There, the following year, they were interred by the Archbishop of Dublin in Whitefriar Street Church, and a shrine to St. Valentine — which has since proved a popular place of prayer for Dublin's luckless romantics — has since emerged on the site.

CHAPTER 6
WORDS & PHRASES

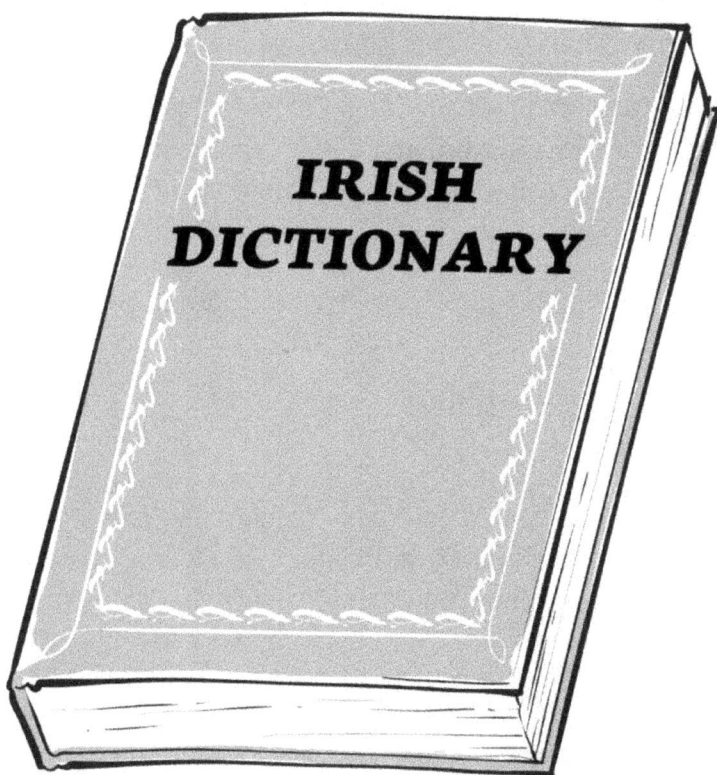

IRISH DICTIONARY

Irish is a beautiful, complex, and heavily nuanced language that — thanks to its roots in the Celtic language family, rather than Germanic or Latin — often looks somewhat impenetrable to English speakers! Nevertheless, English has picked up a great many words from Irish over the years, while the vocabulary of Irish itself has a number of intriguing terms and expressions.

This chapter's quiz looks at some of the most beautiful and bizarre Irish words and phrases.

1. Who or what in Ireland is known as the *Taoiseach*?

    a. Irish Sea
    b. Irish Prime Minister
    c. British monarch
    d. Dublin metro system

2. Where in Ireland might you be most likely to see a *currach*?

    a. In a church
    b. On a dinner table
    c. On an envelope
    d. On water

3. Which of these words is thought to derive from an Irish word meaning "fragments"?

    a. Morsels
    b. Smithereens
    c. Modicums
    d. Jots

4. According to an old Irish proverb, "It's a lonely washing that has no…" what?

    a. "Line to dry it on"
    b. "Man's shirt in it"

c. "Second sock"

d. "Sunny day for it"

5. An Irish person has just said *slán* to you. What are they doing?

   a. Saying hello

   b. Buying you a drink

   c. Asking for your name

   d. Departing

6. As well as meaning a strong accent, what is an Irish *brogue*?

   a. A hat

   b. A shirt

   c. A shoe

   d. A belt

7. *Machree* and *acushla* are notable Irish…what?

   a. Terms of endearment

   b. Insults

   c. Greetings

   d. Culinary dishes

8. According to another Irish proverb, "A lamb's bleat is often more telling than…" what?

   a. "A pig's grunt"

   b. "A dog's bark"

   c. "A cat's meow"

   d. "A bee's buzz"

9. In Ireland and among some Irish people, what is *Shelta*?

   a. Folk music

   b. Traditional dancing

    c. A language

    d. Money

10. What is the (rather appropriate!) literal meaning of the word *leprechaun*, in the sense of an Irish sprite?

    a. "Guardian of the gold"

    b. "Small body"

    c. "Rainbow's end"

    d. "Green attire"

11. What word for an area of waterlogged ground derives from an Irish word meaning "soft"?

    a. Marsh

    b. Bog

    c. Swamp

    d. Bayou

12. In traditional Irish folklore, what woodland creature might be known as a *brock*?

    a. Fox

    b. Squirrel

    c. Hedgehog

    d. Badger

13. Which of these words is thought to derive from an Irish surname?

    a. Hooligan

    b. Thug

    c. Ruffian

    d. Scoundrel

14. In rural Ireland, what is a *turlach*?

a. A bird colony
b. A patch of quicksand
c. A seasonal lake
d. A tree that has been struck by lightning

SOLUTIONS

1. B. Irish Prime Minister. The Irish word *taoiseach* literally means "chief" or "chieftain" but has been used as the title of the Prime Minister of Ireland since the 1930s.

2. D. On water. A *currach*, or *curragh*, is a small animal-hide or canvas boat, similar to a coracle.

3. B. Smithereens. Used in expressions such as "blown to smithereens," the word *smithereens* is thought to descend from the Irish word *smidirin*, literally meaning "little fragment."

4. B. "Man's shirt in it." This old proverb is understood to mean that everyone should find someone to look after or to look after them (and wash their clothes for them!).

5. D. Departing. *Slán*, which essentially means "safety" or "health," is the Irish word for goodbye. It is related to *sláinte*, the Irish drinking toast.

6. C. A shoe. Originally a rough, broad style of shoe made from hide or leather, brogues were once considered so indicative of an Irishman that their name came to be used for the Irish accent—and ultimately, for any noticeable accent or twang—in the 1700s.

7. A. Terms of endearment. *Machree* (a word popularized by the old Irish folk song "Mother Machree") comes from the Irish phrase *mo chroidhe*, meaning "my heart." *Acushla* (popularized more recently in the Hollywood movie *Million Dollar Baby*) comes from the Irish *a chuisle*, literally meaning "pulse" or "heartbeat."

8. B. "A dog's bark." In other words, when someone quietly complains or raises their concern, what they have to say is

often much more important than the complaint of someone habitually brash and noisy!

9. C. A language. *Shelta* began life as a secret and coded language used by Irish traveling tinkers but has since become associated with the idiomatic language of Irish traveling communities as a whole.

10. B. "Small body." In fact, etymologically the word *leprechaun* is thought to be distantly related to the Latin word *corpus*, meaning "body."

11. B. Bog. The word *bog* comes from the Irish *bogach*. In the sense of something that moves flexibly — as the spongy, waterlogged ground is prone to do — it is distantly related to the word *elbow*.

12. D. Badger. The name Brock comes from the Old Irish name for a badger, *brocc*. Through the ancient Celtic population of Anglo-Saxon England, the word was also adopted into Old English and remains in use in a handful of English dialects today as well.

13. A. Hooligan. According to one explanation, *hooligan* comes from the Irish name *Houlihan*, or *O'Hoolighan*, which was popularly used in Victorian music hall songs as the stock name of an Irish comic character.

14. C. A seasonal lake. A *turlach* or *turlough* is a lake that forms in areas of porous bedrock, like the limestone expanses of western Ireland, and so only fills with water when the underlying ground is saturated. The "lach" in *turlach* is distantly related to the word *loch*.

DID YOU KNOW?

One of the best-known words of Irish origin is limerick, the name of a type of five-line poem that takes its name from the Irish city and county of Limerick. The word is thought to derive from an old parlor game once popular in England in which party guests would have to improvise nonsense rhymes starting or including the line "Won't you come up to Limerick?"

THE UNLIKELY SAVIOR OF THE IRISH LANGUAGE

The effects of the Irish famine of the mid-1800s were so great that, by the turn of the century, the native Irish language seemed likely to become extinct. While under British control, all Irish people were required to learn and speak English when dealing with their local authorities. As time went by, English became the more usual language of the island in everyday life. The number of Irish speakers, ultimately, sharply declined.

When Ireland gained home rule and independence in the 1920s, however, the incoming government returned Irish to the forefront: the Irish Constitution lists Irish as the Republic of Ireland's national and first official language, with English listed second. Nevertheless, English remains the most widely spoken language in Ireland, and all government business is conducted in English to this day.

There is, however, still an undercurrent of Irish speakers — and now, in the 21st century, the language is once more picking up in popularity!

Pockets of Irish-speaking communities, in a region known as the *Gaeltacht*, still exist across Ireland, and there, around one-quarter of households — estimated to be somewhere in the region of 30,000 people — profess to be fluent in Irish. In some parts of the *Gaeltacht*, meanwhile, more than 70% of people claim to speak Irish every single day.

Thanks to the sheer number of people with an interest in Irish culture and their Irish bloodline around the world, however, the language continues to strengthen. In 2016, it was reported that a staggering 2.3 million people around the world were using the language-learning app Duolingo to learn Irish. The announcement was so surprising that it prompted a response from the Irish president, Michael Higgins, who arranged for some of the volunteer translators who had overseen the introduction and compilation of the app's Irish program to be honored at a ceremony in Dublin.

With so many people now learning what was once an obscure and endangered language, it now seems likely the Irish language will survive for many years to come!

CHAPTER 7
IRISH FOLKLORE I

From gruesome ghouls to gold-hoarding leprechauns, the folklore and folk traditions of Ireland feature some truly bizarre and extraordinary creatures.

This first chapter of questions dedicated to Irish lore and legend explores some of these creatures, alongside some of the island's mythological kings and queens and folk heroes and heroines.

1. A *banshee* is a creature from Irish folklore that is said to be able to herald someone's death by doing what?

    a. Singing
    b. Screaming
    c. Nodding
    d. Dancing

2. According to tradition, you should decorate your home with crosses made of what on St. Brigid's Day, February 1?

    a. Knots of yarn
    b. Silver foil
    c. Locks of hair
    d. Plaited grasses

3. According to one tale, the legendary Irish hero Finn MacCool, or *Fionn mac Cumhaill*, is popularly associated with the formation of what geographical feature?

    a. The Giant's Causeway
    b. The Atlantic Ocean
    c. Isle of Man
    d. The Irish Sea

4. A tale in Irish and Celtic folklore claims that what fish contains all the knowledge in the world and eating it would impart that knowledge on the diner?

    a. Turbot
    b. Pike
    c. Salmon
    d. Eel

5. Who is the paramour of Diarmuid in a legendary Irish tale of star-crossed lovers?

    a. Colleen
    b. Gráinne
    c. Clodagh
    d. Áine

6. The *Bodach* is a kind of impish trickster or bogeyman in Irish and Celtic folklore, which is often said to take the form of what?

    a. An old man
    b. A black dog
    c. A red-headed girl
    d. A beam of moonlight

7. In Celtic folklore, where might you expect to find a *selkie*?

    a. In a cave
    b. Beneath a tree
    c. On top of a mountain
    d. In the sea

8. As what did the Irish folk heroine Grace O'Malley become known in the 1600s?

a. Pirate

b. Highwaywoman

c. Vigilante

d. Sorceress

9. The Children of Lir is an Irish myth in which a jealous queen transforms her stepchildren into toads. True or False?

   a. True

   b. False

10. The *púca* is a mischievous and sometimes malevolent creature from Irish folklore that supposedly has the magical ability to…what?

    a. Turn invisible

    b. Shapeshift

    c. Reverse time

    d. Grant wishes

11. *Tír na nÓg* is a legendary land in Irish mythology where people remain young forever. Where is it said to be located?

    a. On an island in the far western oceans

    b. In the skies above Galway Bay

    c. Deep below the Ballyhoura Mountains of County Limerick

    d. Below the highest arch of a leprechaun's rainbow

12. Which of these is the name of a renowned warrior queen in Irish folklore?

    a. Mia

    b. Moll

    c. Maeve

    d. Mildred

13. The *Abhartach* is a terrifying creature from Irish folklore that is popularly said to have inspired later stories of what kind of monstrous creature?

    a. Werewolf

    b. Headless Horseman

    c. Vampire

    d. Zombie

14. What metal is said to offer protection against many of the monstrous creatures in Irish myth?

    a. Platinum

    b. Copper

    c. Lead

    d. Iron

SOLUTIONS

1. B. Screaming. The scream, or "keening," of a banshee is said to precede the announcement of a death in Irish folklore. The banshee herself is often described as a withered, ghost-like old woman.
2. D. Plaited grasses. St. Brigid's crosses are typically X-shaped and are neatly woven to create a lozenge-like square knot at their center.
3. A. The Giant's Causeway. According to legend, Finn MacCool built the causeway to use as steppingstones to Scotland, where he intended to do battle with one of his rivals.
4. C. Salmon. *The Salmon of Knowledge* is another tale involving the legendary hero Finn MacCool, who goes in search of the fish in the River Boyne.
5. B. Gráinne. The daughter of an ancient High King of Ireland, Gráinne was originally betrothed to Finn MacCool but secretly eloped with his warrior compatriot Diarmuid instead.
6. A. An old man. Legends of the *Bodach* often also claim him to be the devil himself. The Bodach's female companion, meanwhile, is the Cailleach — an old female sorceress or witch-like being, said to be able to reshape the landscape and conjure up storms and bad weather.
7. D. In the sea. A selkie is a seal-like being that features in countless tales and legends in the mythology of Ireland, Scotland, and Scandinavia.
8. A. Pirate. The pirate queen Gráinne Ní Mháille, or Grace O'Malley, is known to have operated in and overseen trade

in the waters off the west coast of Ireland in the 16th century. Much of her life story is recorded in English, rather than Irish, in historical sources, and in 1593, Grace sailed to London to petition Queen Elizabeth I herself for the release of her sons from captivity!

9. False. In the story, the jealous Queen Aoife transformed her stepchildren—who were the four children of her deceased sister, Eva—into swans.

10. B. Shapeshift. Stories of shapeshifting *púcai* are common across Ireland and other Celtic regions of Europe. In some tales, the *púca* mischievously turns itself into a horse and waits outside a rural tavern. When someone who has had too much to drink stumbles out of the inn, the puca entices them to take a ride on its back then gallops away frenziedly, giving the unfortunate rider a terrifying ordeal before eventually dropping them back off at the tavern where they started!

11. A. On an island in the far western oceans. Said by some storytellers to be a part of the Celtic afterlife, Tír na nÓg is imagined as an island paradise, located far off Ireland's west coast. The name *Tír na nÓg* itself, meanwhile, literally means "land of the young."

12. C. Maeve. Queen Maeve is perhaps best known for a tale in Irish mythology in which she and her husband, Aillil, discuss which of them owns more material things. Not wanting to be bested by her husband, Maeve realizes that Aillil has a grand bull that she does not have among her livestock and so arranges an audacious cattle raid in order to redress the balance!

13. C. Vampire. Often said to have at least in part inspired Bram Stoker's descriptions of Count Dracula, the Abhartach is a dwarf-like creature in Irish folklore said to have inhabited the lands around Slaghtaverty, a small town in Northern Ireland. Having terrorized the local population, the Abhartach was eventually slain and buried upright beneath a hawthorn tree. The following night, however, the creature returned from the grave and began attacking the local people once more. Again, it was slain and buried upright, but a second time it returned from the grave. Only when the Abhartach was buried upside down, with its head facing into the earth, did its devilish hauntings cease.

14. D. Iron. The use of iron to ward off mischievous spirits and fairies or "little people" in Irish legend is one of the reasons why people came to hang horseshoes — which are typically made of iron — above their doors for good luck!

DID YOU KNOW?

The word banshee *is thought to literally mean "fairy-woman" and comes from the Irish equivalent phrase* bean sidhe.

THE STUDENTS' SUPERSTITION

As well as mythical creatures and legendary heroes and heroines, the folklore of Ireland extends to superstitions and traditions that are so ingrained that they are observed by even the most cynical of Irish people. And that is especially true of a tradition surrounding one of the major landmarks of perhaps Ireland's most prestigious universities.

At the center of Library Square, an area of the campus of the famous Trinity College in Dublin, stands the Campanile, a 100ft-tall granite belltower erected in 1853. The grand tower — which was designed by the renowned Victorian architect Sir Charles Lanyon — is topped by a large Corinthian-style belfry, surrounded by stone coats of arms and fitted with a crowning dome.

As beautiful as the tower is, oddly you'll rarely see any students at Trinity College walking the picturesque path that runs beneath it. That's because a longstanding superstition on the campus states that any student who happens to pass below the tower as its bell rings will be destined to fail all their exams!

The tradition holds so firmly, in fact, that many students will only approach the tower and risk walking beneath it on their graduation day — when all their exams are completed — so that whether the tower rings out or not, they can no longer be affected by its bizarre curse!

CHAPTER 8

LITERATURE

Ireland has a long and venerated literary tradition, from early bards and poets to some of the 19th, 20th, and 21st centuries' most popular, admired, and successful writers. For a country of barely five million people, moreover, to date, Ireland has produced no fewer than four Nobel Prize–winning writers: the poets WB Yeats and Seamus Heaney and the playwrights George Bernard Shaw and Samuel Beckett.

This is the first of two sets of questions celebrating anything and everything about Irish literature and Irish writers, past and present.

1. "Bloomsday" is an annual celebration of which famous Irish writer's work?

    a. Samuel Beckett
    b. GB Shaw
    c. Oscar Wilde
    d. James Joyce

2. As well as writing *Gulliver's Travels*, this 17th-century Irish writer was also well known in his day as a satirist and essayist and as a Christian cleric who at one time even served as the Dean of St Patrick's Cathedral, Dublin. Who is he?

    a. Edmund Burke
    b. Jonathan Swift
    c. Oscar Wilde
    d. Oliver Goldsmith

3. "For each man kills the thing he loves, / Yet each man does not die," is a memorable line from what famous Oscar Wilde poem?

a. "Requiescat"

b. "Ravenna"

c. "The Sphinx"

d. "The Ballad of Reading Gaol"

4. The musical *My Fair Lady* is based on what stage play by the Irish dramatist George Bernard Shaw?

    a. *Saint Joan*

    b. *Man and Superman*

    c. *Arms and the Man*

    d. *Pygmalion*

5. What legendary work of literature did the Irish writer Seamus Heaney win worldwide acclaim for his translation of in 1999?

    a. *Beowulf*

    b. *The Iliad*

    c. *Metamorphoses*

    d. *The Odyssey*

6. In Oscar Wilde's famous story *The Picture of Dorian Gray*, where does the title character hide his infamous picture?

    a. In the attic

    b. In a graveyard

    c. On an unused boat

    d. Under his bed

7. With which of the literary arts are the Irish writers Mary Barber, Katharine Tynan, and Eavan Boland most associated?

    a. Journalism

    b. Drama

    c. Poetry

    d. Horror stories

8. *Dracula* author Bram Stoker was born in Clontarf, in Dublin, in 1847. Long before he found fame as a horror writer, however, he worked as a physician at a private medical practice in Cork. True or False?

    a. True
    b. False

9. In the famous opening line of one of WB Yeats' most admired poems, Yeats says "I will arise and go now, and go to…" where?

    a. "Killarney"
    b. "Innisfree"
    c. "Portlaoise"
    d. "Letterkenny"

10. In 1916, James Joyce published his semi-autobiographical novel *A Portrait of the Artist as a…*what?

    a. *Dying Woman*
    b. *Young Man*
    c. *Newborn Baby*
    d. *Lost Boy*

11. What was the title of acclaimed modern Irish author Sally Rooney's debut novel, released in 2017?

    a. *Normal People*
    b. *Intermezzo*
    c. *Conversations with Friends*
    d. *Beautiful World, Where Are You*

12. The 18th–19th-century Irish-born playwright Richard Brinsley Sheridan, best known for his comic plays *The Rivals*

and *The School for Scandal*, once owned what famous building in London?

    a. Buckingham Palace

    b. The National Gallery

    c. Theatre Royal, Drury Lane

    d. The British Museum

13. In what famous novel by an Irish writer would you encounter the characters Lucy Westenra and Jonathan Harker?

    a. *The Life and Opinions of Tristram Shandy, Gentleman*

    b. *Dracula*

    c. *Finnegans Wake*

    d. *Molloy*

14. In what European country did James Joyce die unexpectedly in 1941 and is buried there in Fluntern Cemetery?

    a. Switzerland

    b. Norway

    c. France

    d. Hungary

SOLUTIONS

1. D. James Joyce. Leopold Bloom is the protagonist of Joyce's classic novel *Ulysses*, the events of which take place all on a single day, June 16. "Bloomsday" — which is held on that date — is an annual celebration of Joyce's famous book, as well as his wider works.

2. B. Jonathan Swift. The fantasy adventure *Gulliver's Travels* might be Swift's best-known work today, but in the 1600s, he was just as celebrated for prose works like *A Modest Proposal*, *The Conduct of the Allies*, and — as an ordained clergyman — a famous *Argument Against Abolishing Christianity*. In fact, Swift's full title was The Very Reverend Jonathan Swift.

3. D. "The Ballad of Reading Gaol." Having been found guilty of "gross indecency," Wilde was imprisoned in a Reading jailhouse in 1895 and sentenced to two years' hard labor. He wrote this poem after his release from prison while living in Europe.

4. D. *Pygmalion*. Perhaps Shaw's most celebrated and most produced work, *Pygmalion* was completed in 1913. The story of a lowly flower girl who falls in with a professor who transforms her into a woman of high society was later adapted into the musical *My Fair Lady* in 1956, followed by the Hollywood version starring Audrey Hepburn in 1964.

5. A. *Beowulf*. Heaney's rendition of the Old English epic poem "Beowulf" was published two years after he received the Nobel Prize for Literature in 1995.

6. A. In the attic. Oscar Wilde's terrifying story of a handsome man whose portrait, rather than his own face, comes to

exhibit the effects of his debauched lifestyle is one of the greatest gothic horror novels ever written. Despite "a picture in the attic" becoming a common expression in English, in the story, Wilde never actually calls the place Grey hides his portrait "the attic," but rather describes it merely as a remote and unused upper room in his house.

7. C. Poetry. Mary Barber was one of Ireland's earliest successful female poets and was a member of the same 18th-century literary circle that included Jonathan Swift. Katharine Tynan was a 19th- and early 20th-century poet and contemporary of WB Yeats (who is rumored to have proposed marriage to her but been rejected!). The poet and former Stanford University professor of English Eavan Boland was born in Dublin in 1944 and first began writing poetry after her family moved to England in the 1950s; she later recounted her experiences in one of her most famous and celebrated works, *An Irish Childhood in England: 1951.*

8. False. Stoker's contemporary Arthur Conan Doyle (the creator of Sherlock Holmes) began his career as a doctor, but Stoker was a theatrical agent and famously worked as the personal assistant of the celebrated 19th-century actor Sir Henry Irving.

9. B. "Innisfree." Yeats' poem "The Lake Isle of Innisfree" imagines the writer leaving the hustle and bustle of his life behind and retiring quietly to the island of Innisfree on the southern shore of Lough Gill in Ireland's County Sligo.

10. B. *Young Man.* Joyce's work (which was serialized in 1914–15, before being published for the first time in book form in 1916) introduced the novelist Stephan Dedalus, who Joyce would later return to in his later novel *Ulysses.*

11. C. *Conversations with Friends*. One of the most popular and best-selling Irish novelists of the 21st century, Sally Rooney wrote her first 100,000-word draft of her debut novel *Conversations with Friends* in just three months. Her four novels have now sold more than three million copies worldwide.

12. C. Theatre Royal, Drury Lane. There had been a theater on the corner of Catherine Street and Drury Lane in London's Covent Garden since the 1600s. Sheridan took over the site in 1776 and used it to stage productions of several of his early plays. In 1791, Sheridan demolished the existing playhouse and opened a far larger one on the same site three years later, but sadly it burned down in 1809; the present Drury Lane Theatre opened in 1812.

13. B. *Dracula*. Jonathan Harker is the young English solicitor who is sent to Count Dracula's castle to oversee his affairs before he relocates to London in Bram Stoker's story. Lucy Westenra is Jonathan's fiancée Mina's best friend, who becomes Count Dracula's first victim on his arrival in England.

14. A. Switzerland. Joyce underwent abdominal surgery to treat a perforated ulcer in Zürich in 1941 but never recovered from the procedure and died the following day. Having slipped into a coma, Joyce famously suddenly awoke and asked a nurse to telephone his wife and young son, who were on their way to see him when — just 15 minutes later — he passed away. He was 58 years old.

DID YOU KNOW?

Despite being one of Ireland's most acclaimed authors, James Joyce had terrible eyesight and wrote much of his work on large sheets of paper in bright red crayon. Such was the state of his eyesight, in fact, that he and his wife Nora named their daughter Lucia, after St. Lucia, the patron saint of the blind!

THE BIRTH OF DRACULA

One of the most famous and enduringly popular Irish novels is Bram Stoker's *Dracula*, which was published in 1897. But thanks in part to his close involvement with the London stage, Stoker's most celebrated novel had a rather bizarre route to publication—with Stoker adapting it for the stage *before* it was released to the reading public!

The novel *Dracula* itself was published on May 26, 1897. But just over a week earlier, on May 18 of that year, Stoker unveiled his own stage adaptation of his novel, ostensibly so that audiences could watch the story be performed before reading the book themselves. Stoker seemingly hoped that this stage production—which ran to a full five acts, plus an introductory prologue—would help to drum up interest in his novel and act as a little early publicity.

Unfortunately, the idea did not go entirely as planned: just two people showed up to the debut performance of Stoker's stage play in London's West End!

In Stoker's defense, however, the production was never actually *truly* intended to be a grand show—nor, for that matter, a particularly good one! Knowing that other authors and playwrights might want to adapt his story for the stage once his book *Dracula* had been released, Stoker was keen to secure the dramatic rights to his novel for himself.

As a result, he cobbled together his own stage retelling of the story before publication (and therefore, before anyone else could adapt it themselves) under the title *Dracula, or the Un-*

Dead. Calling on all the contacts he could to bring his production to life, Stoker approached his good friend and employer, the legendary Victorian actor Sir Henry Irving, to see if he was interested in starring in the play as the eponymous count. (Unfortunately, Irving took one look at Stoker's hastily written script and declined, labeling Stoker's stage treatment of the story "dreadful"!)

Nevertheless, production went ahead. But given that Stoker's main priority was a legal one, rather than a financial or artistic one, he put little real effort into redrafts and rehearsals and only began publicizing the performance a half-hour before the curtain went up. Ultimately, just two patrons attended the show.

Whether they then went on to purchase the novel the following week, however, remains unknown!

CHAPTER 9
FOOD AND DRINK

Traditional Irish food includes a great many dishes that are rooted in the animals and produce that have long been reared and grown there. As such, Irish food often features a slice of hearty meat, such as beef, lamb, pork, or mutton, served alongside starchy root crops and other vegetables, including potatoes, turnips, and carrots.

In more recent decades, however, Irish food and drink has expanded widely to include one of the world's most popular beers and a popular twist on a hot cup of coffee! Test your knowledge of Ireland's unique dishes and cuisine with this next set of questions.

1. Which of these meats are you most likely to find in a traditional Irish stew?

   a. Chicken
   b. Fish
   c. Beef
   d. Venison

2. How should an Irish coffee be served?

   a. Mixed through with foamed milk
   b. With a floating layer of cream on top of the black coffee
   c. Mixed with hot chocolate
   d. With a spoonful of melted honey

3. Irish whiskey takes its name from a Gaelic word literally meaning what?

   a. "Water of life"
   b. "Warm draught"

    c. "Drink of the gods"

    d. "Hair of the dog"

4. What kind of food is an Irish *barmbrack*?

    a. Fruited bread roll

    b. Baked custard tart

    c. Meat pie

    d. Fish stew

5. What Irish waterway is famous for its shrimp?

    a. River Shannon

    b. Dublin Bay

    c. Celtic Dea

    d. Lough Foyle

6. What kind of vegetable is an Irish lumper?

    a. Turnip

    b. Carrot

    c. Pumpkin

    d. Potato

7. You're in Ulster and have just been served a *farl*. What are you eating?

    a. A bowl of soup

    b. A hot toddy

    c. A slice of soda bread

    d. A vegetable flan

8. Which of these is the name of a kind of fried potato pancake popular in central Ireland?

    a. Baxter

    b. Bonxie

    c. Boxty

    d. Banjax

9. What is the unlikely main ingredient of a traditional Irish *Timoleague* pudding?

    a. Pigs' blood

    b. Pigs' trotters

    c. Pigs' snouts

    d. Pigs' tails

10. *Poteen* is an Irish vodka-like distilled spirit. But what does its name literally mean?

    a. "Potato liquor"

    b. "Little pot"

    c. "Magic potion"

    d. "Potable liquid"

11. What vegetable is mixed with mashed potato to make a dish of Irish *colcannon*?

    a. Turnip

    b. Beets

    c. Carrots

    d. Cabbage

12. What date is written on the golden harp on the Guinness logo?

    a. 1669

    b. 1759

    c. 1849

    d. 1939

13. What meat is used to make a traditional stew of Irish "skirts and kidneys"?

    a. Pork
    b. Chicken
    c. Beef
    d. Mutton

14. What staple food is boiled with milk, sugar, and spices to make a traditional Irish *goody* dessert?

    a. Rice
    b. Bread
    c. Eggs
    d. Barley

SOLUTIONS

1. C. Beef. Alongside potatoes and other root vegetables, such as carrots or turnips, a traditional Irish stew will typically contain a slice of staple red meat—most often beef, but sometimes lamb.
2. B. With a floating layer of cream on top of the black coffee. Although some variations of Irish coffee mix the cream into the coffee, traditional Irish coffee mixes sugar and whiskey into the freshly brewed coffee, which is then topped off with a floating layer of cold cream. The hot coffee should then be drunk through the cream, not mixed into it.
3. A. "Water of life." Whiskey comes from the Gaelic *uisge beatha*, which is in turn believed to be an Irish or Scots loan translation of the Latin *aqua vita*, meaning "water of life."
4. A. Fruited bread roll. Also known as a *boreen*, or *boreen brack*, a *barmbrack* is a brioche-like sweet bread roll made with raisins or currants. Often made at Halloween, traditionally an item such as a coin or ring would be baked into the mixture, and whoever's barmbrack roll contains it is said to be granted good luck.
5. B. Dublin Bay. This particular kind of shrimp, also known as a Dublin Bay prawn, or *langoustine*, is only found in the seas and inlets of the northeast Atlantic Ocean.
6. D. Potato. The lumper was the potato historically implicated in the widespread infestations in the 1800s that led to the Irish famine. It has waxy flesh and a higher starch content than modern white potatoes.

7. C. A slice of soda bread. Soda bread is typically made into a flat circle and then cut into rounded quarters, known as *farls*. A slice of farl is often served with an Ulster fry, a kind of cooked breakfast featuring bacon, beans, sausages, and blood pudding.

8. C. Boxty. Known in Irish as *bacstaí*, a boxty pancake is made by mixing finely shredded or grated potatoes (or similar root vegetables) with flour and then frying like a pancake.

9. A. Pigs' blood. Like a traditional British black pudding, Irish *Timoleague* or "brown" pudding is made by steeping a mixture of cereal grains and chopped onions in pigs' blood, then boiling the mixture in sausage casings. Slices of the pudding are popularly eaten with Irish-cooked breakfasts.

10. B. Little pot. Once known as "Irish moonshine," poteen was historically brewed at home in small kitchen vessels; hence its name—*poitín* in Irish—derives from the small pans in which it was made.

11. D. Cabbage. Often served on St. Patrick's Day and St. Brigid's Day, *colcannon* is a popular way of using up leftover mashed potatoes in Ireland. When scallions are mixed with potato instead of cabbage, the mixture is called *scamp*.

12. B. 1759. That was the year in which Guinness' inventor, Arthur Guinness, first began brewing stouts and ales at the St. James's Gate Brewery in Dublin.

13. A. Pork. Skirt is the name given to the thin, membranous film of pork meat found around a pig's diaphragm. Despite their meagerness, such offcuts—as well as kidneys and other offal—were once popular in Ireland, at a time when other cuts of meat proved prohibitively expensive. Skirt and kidneys made the most of these ingredients by boiling them

in a hearty stew of onions and potatoes and, traditionally, flavoring it with thyme.

14. B. Bread. *Goody*, or *goodie*, is a traditional Irish bread pudding. It is traditionally prepared on St. John's Eve, June 23, in Ireland, the day before the feast day of St. John the Baptist.

DID YOU KNOW?

Around the world every year, 1.8 billion pints of Guinness are drunk — that's ten million every day!

THE GUINNESS FACTORY'S EXTRAORDINARY LEASE

Although it might sound like a fictitious story, Guinness stout is indeed named after its inventor, a genuine Dublin Irish brewer named Arthur Guinness, who first began producing his namesake drink in the city more than 250 years ago.

Guinness was born in County Kildare in 1725, into a family with close ties to the Archbishop of Cashel, a town in nearby County Tipperary. (It seems likely, in fact, that Arthur was named in honor of the archbishop, whose name was Arthur Price!) Arthur Guinness' father worked as the archbishop's land steward, and as part of his employment, he was involved in overseeing the breweries that operated on the bishop's property. It was likely through this work that a young Arthur Guinness was first introduced to the art of brewing.

When the archbishop died, he left Arthur £100 in his will, which he used to set up his first brewery in the town of Leixlip, on the outskirts of Dublin. As the business grew, Arthur looked to expand into the city of Dublin itself and eventually secured a now-famous spot in an established brewery in the St. James's Gate area of the city. This grand site had many of the necessary fixtures and fittings already installed, and it covered a total of four acres of land—perfect for expanding his business. All Arthur needed to do was secure a competitive enough lease to allow him to ply his trade in the city for a long time to come. And boy, did Arthur manage it!

At the age of just 34, Arthur used all his savvy business skills to arrange with the city of Dublin a 9,000-year lease—paid at an annual rate of just £45 every 12 months. With the financial pressures now eased and the length of his tenure in Dublin now all but guaranteed, Arthur could throw all his efforts into his new brewery. By the following decade, he had become one of the most successful brewers in all of Ireland.

It was in the late 1770s that Guinness began brewing the now iconic black porter that bears his name today, and it was in 1796 that the first overseas shipment of Guinness beer left Ireland's shores and it began to be sold globally for the first time.

Wisely, Guinness began tweaking his recipe, producing slightly different beers and stouts dependent on how long the liquor would have to be stored on board ships, which was, in turn, dependent on how distant the market it was to be sold in was from Ireland. As a result, Guinness began developing distinct East India beer, as well as varieties suitable for sale in the Caribbean islands, and even Africa; many of these recipes and varieties of Guinness continue to be sold in these separate global markets to this day. With people drinking Guinness beers all over the world, his business was thriving, and by the late 1800s, the St. James's Gate site was the largest brewery on the planet!

Today, incredibly, Arthur Guinness' 9,000-year lease still stands and remains valid. So, thanks to Arthur's canny business skills, his hugely popular stout—which continues to be drank all over the world—will be produced in the city of Dublin for a long time to come!

CHAPTER 10
DUBLIN

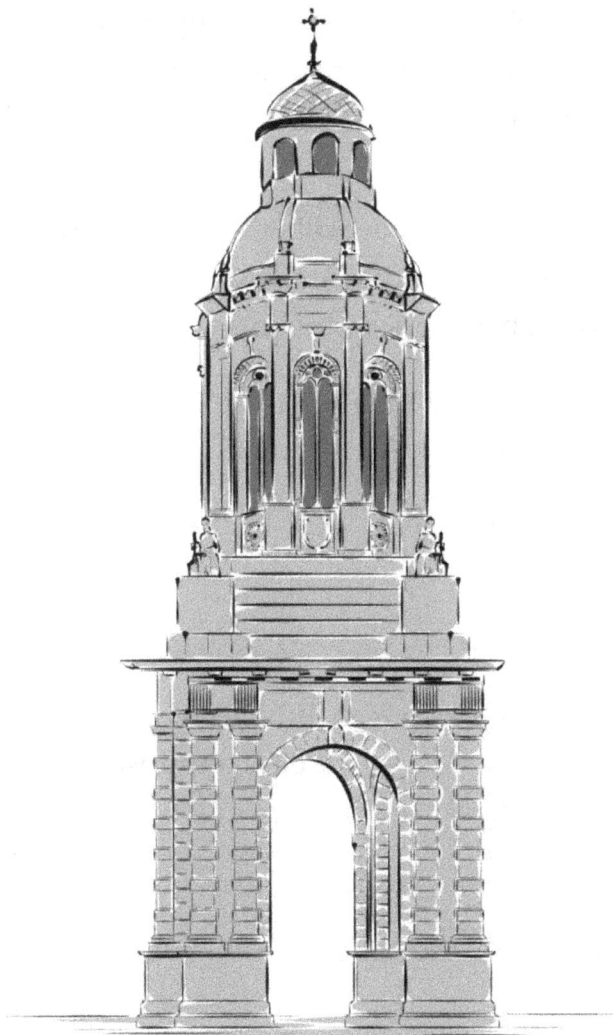

The city of Dublin has a long and varied history, dating far back to ancient Celtic Ireland. It was then that this otherwise unassuming location, at a quiet river mouth on the Irish coast, was first established as the *Dubhlinn*—a name that literally means "black pool." Over the centuries, this city has grown and grown, so that today the entire city and its suburbs boast a population of well over one million people—far beyond that of any other Irish city; in fact, Ireland's second-largest city, Cork, has a population of just over 200,000, barely a fifth of that of the capital!

This next set of questions will test your knowledge of this fascinating and colorful city, its long history, and some of its most intriguing characters and claims to fame.

1. What is the name of the river that flows through Dublin and empties into the Irish Sea?

    a. Shannon
    b. Liffey
    c. Barrow
    d. Nore

2. Dublin's iconic O'Connell Bridge, which connects the two north and south sides of the city, comprises how many stone arches or "spans"?

    a. Three
    b. Six
    c. Nine
    d. 12

3. Dublin has a famous park that shares its name with what mythical creature?

a. Centaur

b. Griffin

c. Sphinx

d. Phoenix

4. What is the name of Ireland's national theater, located in the center of the city of Dublin?

   a. The Abbey

   b. The Nunnery

   c. The Monastery

   d. The Church

5. The Brazen Head is reputed to be the oldest building of its kind in all of Dublin. What is it?

   a. A hotel

   b. A newsagent

   c. A hospital

   d. A pub

6. The library of Dublin's renowned Trinity College is home to the *Book of Kells* — a 9th-century manuscript containing what?

   a. An early Irish dictionary

   b. The Gospels

   c. Medicinal cures and remedies

   d. A map of Ireland

7. Which of these is the name of a region on the outskirts of Dublin?

   a. The Liberties

   b. The Freedoms

   c. The Emancipations

   d. The Sovereignties

8. What is the name of the Irish parliament, which meets in Leinster House in Dublin?

    a. Dáil

    b. Gáil

    c. Sáil

    d. Háil

9. Dublin's Glasnevin Cemetery is known for its high walls and surrounding series of tall towers—the purpose of which was…what?

    a. To provide homes for gravediggers

    b. To deter body snatchers

    c. To count mourners

    d. To sell flowers

10. An annual performance of what famous piece of classical music is held in the cultural Temple Bar region of Dublin?

    a. Handel's *Messiah*

    b. Mozart's *Requiem*

    c. Bizet's *Carmen*

    d. Beethoven's 5th Symphony

11. Dublin's famous Shelbourne Hotel has a distant and bizarre connection to an unlikely figure from European history. Who?

    a. Josef Stalin

    b. Adolf Hitler

    c. Jack the Ripper

    d. Benito Mussolini

12. Dublin's Rotunda Hospital is reported to be the first hospital in Europe to have been built exclusively to treat…who?

a. Children

b. Older people

c. New mothers

d. Injured soldiers

13. According to legend, which of these phrases is thought to have once referred to a region around Dublin?

    a. Beyond the pale

    b. Big fish in a small pond

    c. In cahoots

    d. Cut to the chase

14. During Dublin's Easter Rising in 1916, what kind of building served as the makeshift headquarters of the leaders of the uprising?

    a. Barroom

    b. Post office

    c. General store

    d. Garage

SOLUTIONS

1. B. Liffey. At 82 miles in length, the Liffey is one of Ireland's longest rivers — but is barely a third of the length of the longest overall, the Shannon, which flows for over 220 miles across the country.

2. A. Three. Built on the site of the older Carlisle Bridge, which had joined the two halves of the city of Dublin since the 1700s, O'Connell Bridge was completed in 1882. It was at that point that it was named after the Catholic liberation activist Daniel O'Connell.

3. D. Phoenix. The name "Phoenix" Park is actually an anglicized form of the Irish word *fhionnuisce*, meaning an area of clear, still water — and so has nothing to do with mythical birds!

4. A. The Abbey. Dublin's Abbey Theatre, the National Theatre of Ireland, opened in 1904 and was the first state-subsidized theatre in the English-speaking world.

5. D. A pub. Although the current Brazen Head inn opened in the 1690s as a coaching inn, the site has reputedly been in use since medieval times.

6. B. The Gospels. Created in Ireland (or, according to some accounts, Scotland) sometime around 800 CE, the *Book of Kells* is an illuminated Celtic Latin rendering of the Gospels and also contains several other shorter works of prose and literature.

7. A. The Liberties. The area was so named during the British control of Ireland, as the area was outside the city and therefore not subject to the rules of the king or the crown.

8. A. Dáil. The *Dáil Éireann,* or Assembly of Ireland, is the lower political house of the Irish legislature (or *Oireachtas*) and sits alongside the senate (*Seanad*) and the office of the Irish president (*Uachtarán*).

9. B. To deter body snatchers. The resting place of many of Ireland's most famous figures, including Michael Collins and Daniel O'Connell, Glasnevin Cemetery was opened in 1832. Its surrounding watchtowers and turrets were built as a deterrent to would-be body snatchers who might seek to steal from or dig up those who are buried there.

10. A. Handel's *Messiah.* George Frideric Handel's *Messiah* oratorio was first performed on Fishamble Street in Temple Bar on April 13, 1742. This annual concert commemorates the city's connection to one of the world's and classical music's most famous composers.

11. B. Adolf Hitler. Incredibly, Hitler's brother Alois once worked as a waiter in the restaurant at the Shelbourne Hotel!

12. C. New mothers. In fact, the original and official name for the Rotunda is the "Hospital for the Relief of Poor Lying-in Women."

13. A. Beyond the pale. The "pale" in the phrase *beyond the pale* has nothing to do with having pallid skin but is the word for a fence post used to mark a boundary line. The phrase itself is said to date back to the Middle Ages when a line of pales was used to mark out the boundary around the part of Ireland under English control. Anywhere "beyond the pale" ultimately lay outside of this area of jurisdiction.

14. B. Post office. The Irish teacher and nationalist activist Patrick Henry Pearse read out the official Proclamation of

the Irish Republic outside of a post office in Dublin on April 24, 1916.

DID YOU KNOW?

Dublin has been home to so many writers and literary giants over the years that visitors can enjoy a literary pub crawl, popping in for a drink in a series of pubs and bars, each of which was the favorite haunt of one of the city's greatest writers!

In fact, Dublin has such a proud literary history that it is one of just over 50 official UNESCO Cities of Literature in the world — alongside the likes of Edinburgh, Milan, Québec, Barcelona, and Nanjing.

THE CLOCK THAT COUNTED DOWN TO NOTHING

In 1996, arrangements were made for a vast seven-digit clock to be installed on the riverbed below Dublin's famous O'Connell Bridge, which would tick down the number of seconds remaining until the year 2000. The clock—which was partly funded by the Irish National Lottery—was to become a major attraction in the center of Dublin city, as well as form a centerpiece of Dublin's millennium celebrations.

Unfortunately, things did not quite go as planned. Unveiled in March 1996, by the winter of the same year, the clock had become so obscured by mud, silt, and algae that it could barely be seen on the riverbed, never mind used to tell the time remaining in the 20th century! Mechanical problems, too, began to affect the clock's accuracy, and with upkeep and cleaning costs now seemingly untenable, the clock was removed in December 1996, less than a year after it was installed—and over three years ahead of schedule!

By then, the clock, which, in characteristically humorous Irish style, became known locally as "The Chime in the Slime," had become something of an embarrassment for the local council, and so all vestiges of it were set to be removed. That included the clock's control panel, which had been embedded into the stonework on O'Connell Bridge itself. Its removal left a large, rectangular rubbly depression in the bridge's otherwise pristine stonework, of which local pranksters, in similarly characteristically humorous style, were only too quick to take advantage.

In 2004, several years after the control panel's removal, visitors to Dublin noticed that a formal bronze plaque had been installed in its place, celebrating the life of a local clergyman named Father Pat Noise. "This plaque commemorates Fr. Pat Noise," the text on it read, explaining that Father Noise was once an "advisor to Peadar Clancey." Apparently, the clergyman had "died under suspicious circumstances" when his horse-drawn carriage plunged off the side of O'Connell Bridge and into the river below on August 10, 1919.

The plaque was professionally cast and made of solid bronze; it was estimated that manufacturing and installing it must have run more than €1,000 (over $1,200 at the time).

Despite the rather formal and professional nature of the plaque, when its installation and appearance were investigated by the local council and the police, it became clear that "Father Pat Noise" was entirely made up, and no such accident in 1919 had ever taken place. The plaque was a complete hoax!

Who—and for that matter, why—had someone gone to all the effort to install the plaque, despite "Father Pat Noise" being a complete fabrication? Two years later, in 2006, the two anonymous pranksters behind the Pat Noise plaque came forward to the press, giving video proof of them installing the plaque in 2004. The men's identities were kept secret, but they claimed that the plaque was an inside joke intended to commemorate their own father. The name "Pat Noise," meanwhile, had been nothing more than a play on *paternoster*, the Latin name for the Lord's Prayer.

When the story broke in the press, Dublin council announced that the plaque was to be immediately removed, as its installation had obviously been unauthorized. In response, several locals left floral tributes at the site — where, a year later, it mysteriously reappeared once again.

For a second time, plans were made to remove the plaque to make way for renovations on the O'Connell Bridge — only this time, the joke had by now become so well established in the Dublin community that even some local councilors objected to its removal. So, after the renovations on the bridge were completed, the plaque remained in place.

The mysterious plaque to Father Noise remains in situ to this day, delighting local Dubliners — and no doubt puzzling visitors who are not in on the gag!

CHAPTER 11
IRISH MUSIC II

From centuries-old folk ballads to Grammy-winning international rock stars, this second round of questions dedicated to music covers anything and everything the Irish music world has to offer.

Can you score a perfect 14/14?

1. Which Irish rock band's 1993 debut album, *Everybody Else Is Doing It, So Why Can't We?* featured the hit singles "Linger" and "Dreams"?

    a. The Cranberries
    b. The Chieftains
    c. The Corrs
    d. Hothouse Flowers

2. What was the title of Enya's 1988 breakthrough album, which featured the worldwide smash hit single "Orinoco Flow"?

    a. *Waterfall*
    b. *Waterway*
    c. *Watershed*
    d. *Watermark*

3. What does musician Larry Mullen, Jr., typically play in the rock band U2?

    a. Guitar
    b. Bass
    c. Piano
    d. Drums

4. What town, some 50 miles outside of Dublin, completes the title of the popular Irish folk ballad, "Follow Me Up to…"?

a. Tralee

b. Athlone

c. Carlow

d. Dundalk

5. Which member of the pop group One Direction was born in Ireland?

   a. Zayn Malik

   b. Harry Styles

   c. Louis Tomlinson

   d. Niall Horan

6. "Guess who just got back today?" is the opening line of what classic track by an Irish rock act?

   a. "Where The Streets Have No Name"

   b. "Brown Eyed Girl"

   c. "Salvation"

   d. "The Boys Are Back in Town"

7. Sinéad O'Connor's 1990 breakout album was called *I Do Not Want What*...?

   a. ...*I Don't Need*

   b. ...*I Haven't Got*

   c. ...*You've Given Me*

   d. ...*I Can't See*

8. Moya Brennan, the founding member and vocalist in the Irish New Age act Clannad, is related to the Irish music superstar Enya. How?

   a. They're mother and daughter

   b. They're sisters

   c. They're cousins

   d. Their husbands are brothers

9. *Moondance* was a 1970 album by which Irish artist?

   a. Van Morrison
   b. Rory Gallagher
   c. Phil Lynott
   d. Luke Kelly

10. Which of these classic U2 albums was partly made up of live recordings from the band's *The Joshua Tree* tour in 1987?

    a. *Achtung Baby*
    b. *Rattle and Hum*
    c. *The Unforgettable Fire*
    d. *October*

11. Which British singer—who had a Top 5 hit in the US with "Walking Down Madison"—duetted with Irish rock band The Pogues on the classic Christmas single "Fairytale of New York"?

    a. Kate Bush
    b. Sheena Easton
    c. Kirsty MacColl
    d. Kim Wilde

12. Irish singer Róisín Murphy provided the vocals for what song by the pop dance act Moloko, which was a worldwide hit in 1999?

    a. "Going Back"
    b. "Bring It Back"
    c. "Dancing Back"
    d. "Sing It Back"

13. What 2001 track by Enya became inadvertently associated with that year's 9/11 terrorist attacks in New York when

several news stations played it over footage of the attack's aftermath?

    a. "On My Way Home"
    b. "Anywhere Is"
    c. "Book of Days"
    d. "Only Time"

14. In the lyrics to the famous Irish folk song "Molly Malone," what does Molly cry out as she walks the streets of Dublin?

    a. "Cockles and mussels!"
    b. "Chicken and bacon!"
    c. "Gammon and spinach!"
    d. "Fresh bread and butter!"

SOLUTIONS

1. A. The Cranberries. The album and its singles proved a smash hit worldwide, with *Everybody Else Is Doing It, So Why Can't We?* remaining on the Billboard album chart for almost two years!

2. D. *Watermark*. The album sold 11 million copies worldwide, including four million in the United States alone.

3. D. Drums. Dublin-born Larry Mullen, Jr., joined U2 when the band formed in 1976 and has played drums on all their albums since.

4. C. Carlow. The song makes mention of the English queen Elizabeth I and celebrates the Irish troops' victory at the Battle of Glenmalure in 1580.

5. D. Niall Horan. Horan was born in Mullingar, in County Westmeath, central Ireland, in 1993.

6. D. "The Boys Are Back in Town." One of Thin Lizzy's most popular tracks, "The Boys Are Back in Town" was a global smash hit in 1976, reaching the Top 20 of the US Billboard charts and the Top 10 in the UK.

7. B. *...I Haven't Got.* Featuring hits such as "Nothing Compares 2 U" and "The Emperor's New Clothes," *I Do Not Want What I Haven't Got* was Sinéad O'Connor's second album. It received critical acclaim and sold more than seven million copies around the world.

8. B. They're sisters. In fact, Clannad comprises several members of Enya's family, and she began her musical career as a member of the band before going solo in the early 1980s. Like her sister, Moya (or Máire) Brennan has been

nominated for several Grammy Awards, but she is perhaps best known for her contributions to the soundtrack to James Cameron's movie *Titanic*.

9. A. Van Morrison. *Moondance* was Morrison's third album, following his smash debut *Blowin' Your Mind!* in 1967, and its 1968 follow-up *Astral Weeks*.

10. B. *Rattle and Hum*. Alongside hit singles like "Desire" and "When Love Comes to Town," *Rattle and Hum* featured live cover recordings of several classic songs by other artists, including Bob Dylan's "All Along the Watchtower" and the Beatles' "Helter Skelter."

11. C. Kirsty MacColl. "Fairytale of New York" was only a minor hit on its first release in 1987, although it briefly made the UK Top 10 and hit Number 1 in the Pogues' native Ireland. Since then, however, with digital sales and streaming figures now included in official chart figures, it has routinely resurfaced every Christmas and has consistently recharted every year since 2005!

12. D. "Sing It Back." The track hit Number 1 on the US Billboard Dance charts and in 2022 was ranked by *Rolling Stone* magazine as one of the top dance tracks of all time.

13. D. "Only Time." After the song became so unexpectedly attached to the events of the September 11 attacks, Enya donated the total royalty earnings from the single—which eventually hit the Top 10 on the Billboard chart—to the Uniformed Firefighters Association Widows' and Children's Fund, which aided the families of firefighters killed or injured in the attacks.

14. A. "Cockles and mussels!" Or more fully, Molly Malone calls out, "Cockles and mussels, alive, alive-o!" The song—which

tells the story of a young fishwife plying her trade from a wheelbarrow on the streets of Dublin — dates back to the late 1800s, although popular legend claims it to be based on a real fishwife who may have worked in Dublin as far back as the 17th century.

DID YOU KNOW?

Despite its association with Ireland, the earliest record of the song "Molly Malone" was printed in New England, in Boston, in 1876.

THE STORY OF JIMMY MURPHY

Ireland has a long tradition of folk songs and folk music, with even the national anthem of Ireland being based on an old traditional melody. But of all Ireland's folk tunes, among the most bizarre is the song "Jimmy Murphy," or "Little Jimmy Murphy," whose origins lie somewhere in the 19th century.

According to at least one version of the song's roots, "Jimmy Murphy" emerged among music hall entertainers sometime in the Victorian era. Its lyrics — in some versions at least, as several alternatives exist — in part reference the infamous Irish Rebellion of 1798, in which Irish republican forces rose against the ruling Great British forces mainly around the southeast of Ireland, in County Kildare, County Wicklow, and County Wexford. "As I walked through Kildare while the great rout was ragin'," the song begins, "Little Jimmy Murphy was the lad who was taken." At least one account of the song's origins, meanwhile, claims these lyrics were written or at least passed on by a soldier who was present at the fighting in County Kildare.

Songs inspired by political upheaval and unrest are by no means new, of course, and in the music hall era it was common for songs to address current affairs, make contemporary references, and comment (often satirically) on recent historical and political events. What makes this song so different, however, is that the chorus-like refrain of "Little Jimmy Murphy" is a string of complete nonsense.

"There died little Jimmy Murphy on the sweet mossy banks," the song continues, "Killa-ma-jing, Killa-maj-ong, Whiskey fiskey tooraloo / Rank a diddle dare, Ol' foldare, ol' foldoe!"

Precisely what those lines—which are repeated several times throughout the entire song—are meant to mean is anyone's guess. Are they just musical fillers meant to be replaced at a later date with more meaningful words? Or is it a case that the soldier who passed on this tune (if indeed *that* story is accurate!) was speaking Irish to an Englishman, or else perhaps had such a strong accent that his words could not be written down correctly? As a result, the song's refrain became a string of syllables intended to do little more than fill out the melody and flesh out the line.

Whatever these nonsense lines are meant to be, the song has now remained popular for almost two centuries, with versions still recorded by Irish folk artists and music groups to this day.

CHAPTER 12
IRISH HISTORY II

Time to take another journey into Ireland's long and storied past with this second set of questions on Irish history. From the Viking raids of antiquity to the political turmoil of the 1900s, this chapter will take you on a quizzing journey through more than a millennium of events and upheaval!

1. In what year did the dual passing of a series of *Acts of Union* in both the British and Irish parliaments legally unite the two nations as the United Kingdom of Great Britain and Ireland for the first time?

   a. 1500
   b. 1600
   c. 1700
   d. 1800

2. A longtime muse of the poet WB Yeats, the Irish revolutionary Maud Gonne achieved great success outside of politics as a what?

   a. Pianist
   b. Sculptor
   c. Actress
   d. Dancer

3. Which ancient invaders of the island of Ireland established fortresses known as *longphorts*, or *longphuirt*, along the Irish coastline?

   a. Normans
   b. Angles
   c. Vikings
   d. Romans

4. Which Irish city was for 600 years ruled over by a select band of merchant families, known as the "Tribes" of the city?

    a. Kilkenny
    b. Limerick
    c. Dublin
    d. Galway

5. In the mid-1990s, the Republic of Ireland had a noticeable economic boom that became known worldwide as…what?

    a. The Eire Cat
    b. The Celtic Tiger
    c. The Irish Lion
    d. The Dublin Leopard

6. What was the name of the Irish revolutionary figure who was killed in an ambush during the Irish Civil War while stopped at a remote crossroads outside Béal na Bláth, a village near Bandon in County Cork, in 1922?

    a. Séamus Dwyer
    b. Michael Collins
    c. Larry Griffin
    d. Patrick McCarry

7. After English control of Ireland faltered during the Wars of the Roses, which English king resolved to reconquer Ireland and bring it back under England's control in 1536?

    a. Richard III
    b. Henry VIII
    c. Elizabeth I
    d. James I

8. What town on the outskirts of Dublin—now an affluent suburb of the capital—is known as the site of a decisive battle between the legendary High King of Ireland Brian Boru and the Vikings in 1014?

    a. Clontarf
    b. Rush
    c. Bray
    d. Greystones

9. In what Irish city is Reginald's Tower, a renowned Anglo-Norman castle tower built in the 13th century?

    a. Cork
    b. Limerick
    c. Galway
    d. Waterford

10. In what century did the plague reach Ireland?

    a. 9th century
    b. 11th century
    c. 14th century
    d. 16th century

11. During the persecution of Catholics in Ireland in the mid-1600s, the English parliamentarian leader Oliver Cromwell arranged for many thousands of Catholics from across Ireland to be forced into servitude and transported as slaves. Where were they sent?

    a. France
    b. Australia
    c. Turkey
    d. The Caribbean

12. What is the name of the Irish political party—whose name means "we ourselves" in Irish—which was founded in 1905 as a socialist republican party overseeing Ireland's march toward independence from Britain?

    a. Fine Gael
    b. Sinn Féin
    c. Fianna Fáil
    d. Éirígí

13. Which of these hugely important British figures of the 18th and 19th centuries was—despite his ties to England—actually born in Dublin in 1769?

    a. William Gladstone
    b. The Duke of Wellington
    c. Admiral Nelson
    d. Captain Cook

14. In 1979, Lord Mountbatten—a major British statesman and decorated naval officer—was assassinated by Irish republican forces while sailing off the coast of Ireland. To which member of Britain's royal family was he most closely related?

    a. George V
    b. Queen Elizabeth II
    c. Prince Philip, Duke of Edinburgh
    d. Princess Diana

SOLUTIONS

1. D. 1800. Although another *Act of Union* had united Scotland and England in 1701, it was the *Acts of Union* of 1800 that united the newly formed kingdom of Great Britain with Ireland. *The Acts* remained in force until Ireland's independence in the 1920s, and in the Republic of Ireland today, at least, have now been fully repealed.

2. C. Actress. Gonne's life was an extraordinarily varied and dramatic one: as well as achieving notoriety as both an actress and a revolutionary figurehead, she was also a journalist and essayist, an occultist, and a mystic — as well as proving a real-life inspiration for one of Ireland's greatest ever writers.

3. C. Vikings. The Vikings first arrived in Ireland in the late 8th century, but it was in 852 that they came to Dublin Bay and built a fortress from which to operate a more permanent Irish base. As more of these coastal fortresses appeared, they became known as *longphorts* — a word meaning "ship encampments" in Old Irish.

4. D. Galway. The Tribes of Galway, as they were known, were the Athy, Blake, Bodkin, Browne, D'Arcy, Deane, Font, French, Joyce, Kirwan, Lynch, Martin, Morris, and Skerritt families, who ruled over the city from the 13th to the 19th centuries. Showing just how far back these ancient dynasties can be traced, all but two of these 14 "tribes" are descended from ancient Norman Irish invaders.

5. B. The Celtic Tiger. In the 1990s, Ireland greatly benefited from increased overseas funding and investment — much of

it channeled through the European Union, of which Ireland had been a founding member back in 1993.

6. B. Michael Collins. A government minister in the parliament of the self-declared Irish Free States, Collins had served as the Director of Intelligence of the Irish Republican Army. His support of a new Anglo–Irish treaty, which furthered Ireland's independence but made a condition of an oath of allegiance to the British Crown, led to his death at the hands of anti-treaty campaigners in August 1922.

7. B. Henry VIII. King Henry's plan to retake Ireland for England took almost 70 years to complete, as it was continually thwarted by strong local resistance and infighting. Henry launched his campaign in 1536, but it would not be until 1603 — some 56 years after his death — that all of Ireland would once again come under English rule.

8. A. Clontarf. The decisive Battle of Clontarf, in which King Brian Boru was victorious, is seen as the beginning of the end of Viking settlement in Ireland.

9. D. Waterford. The 54-ft tower is the oldest civic building in all of Ireland.

10. C. 14th century. The first recorded case of the Black Death in Ireland was in 1348.

11. D. The Caribbean. In a chapter of Irish history that is all too often overlooked today, Oliver Cromwell personally oversaw the forced removal and indentured servitude of some 12,000 Irish Catholics, the majority of whom were sent to work as slaves in plantations on the island of Barbados.

12. B. Sinn Féin. Originally a single party, the disagreements surrounding Irish independence in 1922 and Ireland's future relationship with its former controlling force, Great Britain,

led to several breakaway factions. Fine Gael (originally known as *Cumann na nGaedheal*, the "Society of the Gaels") broke away from Sinn Féin in 1923, while Fianna Fáil followed in 1926.

13. B. The Duke of Wellington. A hero of the Napoleonic and Peninsular Wars, Arthur Wellesley, the 1st Duke of Wellington, was born into an aristocratic Anglo–Irish family in Dublin. During his two terms as British prime minister in the early 1800s, Wellesley sought to do right by his Irish roots by forcing through the *Irish Catholic Relief Act* of 1829, which essentially removed the bars that had until then prevented Roman Catholics from serving in parliament and other civic and judicial roles.

14. C. Prince Philip, Duke of Edinburgh. Lord Mountbatten was Prince Philip's maternal uncle.

DID YOU KNOW?

Newgrange is a neolithic monument in Ireland's County Meath that was built sometime around 3200 BCE—making it older than both Stonehenge and the Pyramids!

THE MYSTERY OF BALLYCOTTON IRELAND

Given it's a place steeped in magic and folklore, it is perhaps unsurprising that the history of Ireland includes several unsolved mysteries. One such famous tale involves the mysterious island off the coast of Ballycotton, in County Cork. It appeared out of the mist one morning in the harbor there, before vanishing again into the ether as soon as the local fisherman attempted to sail out to it.

Another mystery surrounds the famous racehorse Shergar, which was "horse-napped" from its yard in Ireland in 1983 and ransomed by its abductors for £2 million. The ransom was never paid, and Shergar's fate—as well as the identities of his kidnappers—remains unknown.

In more recent years, however, one story that has caused something of a stir in Ireland is the so-called "Vanishing Circle"—Ireland's own criminal version of the Bermuda Triangle.

It was in the 1990s that police first began investigating a series of mysterious disappearances of women in the Leinster region of Ireland. When these disappearances were mapped, the locations of the women's final known sightings formed a vaguely circular shape—something like a squashed and rounded triangle—linking Louth, Offaly, and Wexford.

As time went on, the number of cases continued to rise, with a total of eight women, all of similar ages, reported missing. Their disappearances fueled speculation that a serial killer or kidnapper might be on the loose in rural southern Ireland—and, true enough, in 2001 a man accused of the assault and attempted murder of a young woman was arrested in the nearby Wicklow Mountains.

Although the disappearances stopped around the same time as the man's arrest, he has never actually confessed to any of the other crimes or disappearances to which he has been only conspiratorially linked. Were the other mysterious disappearances down to him too, or was there another killer (or killers) at work who had gone into hiding? Or did this bizarre clutch of disappearances comprise distinct cases, with only coincidental connections between them? Whatever the case, Ireland's Vanishing Circle remains unsolved to this day.

CHAPTER 13
SPORTS AND GAMES

Over the years, Ireland has produced world-class rugby stars, athletes, Olympians, and world-champion boxers. But at home, Ireland's national sports are the decidedly local and quintessentially Irish pursuits of Gaelic football and hurling. Together with several other native Irish sports, these comprise the Gaelic Games—a series of Irish-origin sports, several of which are overseen on a professional level by Ireland's unique sporting organization, the Gaelic Athletic Association (GAA).

Showing just how old Ireland's love affair with sport is—and just how popular these sports and games are—the GAA was founded way back in 1884. But how much do you know about Irish sports and games?

1. The Curragh and Fairyhouse are famous Irish locations in what sport?

    a. Hockey
    b. Horse racing
    c. Soccer
    d. Athletics

2. How many players are there on a Gaelic football team?

    a. 8
    b. 11
    c. 15
    d. 21

3. Croke Park is the name of a major sports stadium in Ireland. In what city is it located?

    a. Cork
    b. Galway

c. Dublin

d. Kilkenny

4. *Caid* is an ancient Celtic ball sport that is most similar in play and action to what modern-day game?

   a. Tennis

   b. Rugby

   c. Cricket

   d. Golf

5. Ireland's Kellie Harrington is a two-time Olympic women's gold medalist in what sport?

   a. Diving

   b. Boxing

   c. Fencing

   d. Shooting

6. Which of these is the name of a women's form of the game of hurling?

   a. Camaraderie

   b. Camstone

   c. Camogie

   d. Camboge

7. What might an Irish sportsperson be most likely to do with a *sliotar*?

   a. Hit it

   b. Wear it

   c. Run around it

   d. Jump over it

8. True or False? In Gaelic football, the ball can be thrown *or* kicked into the goal's mouth to score a point.

   a. True
   b. False

9. With what team sport are Irish international legends Brian O'Driscoll and Johnny Sexton associated?

   a. Soccer
   b. Cricket
   c. Baseball
   d. Rugby union

10. Which world champion boxer defeated Irish mixed martial artist Conor McGregor in a notorious crossover match held in Nevada in 2017?

    a. Manny Pacquiao
    b. Floyd Mayweather, Jr.
    c. Miguel Cotto
    d. Oscar De La Hoya

11. On his way to winning the 2011 US Open at Congressional Country Club in Bethesda, Maryland, Northern Irish golfer Rory McIlroy made history when he attained what score during the competition's third round, becoming the first player ever to record it?

    a. –8 under par
    b. –10 under par
    c. –12 under par
    d. –14 under par

12. The goal in a game of Gaelic football is H-shaped, with a horizontal crossbar linking the two uprights. A team scores

one point if they successfully pass the ball *over* the crossbar and into the goal—but how many points do they score if the ball passes *under* the crossbar and into the goal?

   a. 0
   b. 2
   c. 3
   d. 6

13. In what sport was Ireland's Sonia O'Sullivan a World Champion and Olympic silver medalist?

   a. Gymnastics
   b. Swimming
   c. Athletics
   d. Archery

14. By what epithet is the Irish hockey-like sport of hurling sometimes known?

   a. "The fastest sport in the world"
   b. "The loudest sport in the world"
   c. "The oldest sport in the world"
   d. "The most dangerous sport in the world"

SOLUTIONS

1. B. Horse racing. The Curragh in particular plays host to all five of Ireland's Classics flat races—namely the Irish 1,000 Guineas, the Irish 2,000 Guineas, the Irish Derby, the Irish Oaks, and the Irish St. Leger.

2. C. 15. Each Gaelic football team comprises six backs, two midfielders, six forwards, and a goalkeeper.

3. C. Dublin. Originally opened in the 1880s, Croke Park has been greatly expanded over the years and today seats more than 80,000 people. It is the home of both Gaelic sports in Ireland and the Irish national stadium.

4. B. Rugby. In fact, *caid* (which is often used as an umbrella term for lots of similar sports) is seen by some historians as the ancient precursor to Gaelic football.

5. B. Boxing. Harrington took gold in the women's lightweight division in both the 2020 Tokyo Games and the 2024 Paris Games.

6. C. Camogie. The game takes its name from the Irish word *camógaíocht*, meaning "little stick"—a reference to the hockey-like stick the players use to strike the ball.

7. A. Hit it. The *sliotar* is the hard leather baseball-like ball used in bat-and-ball games like shinty and hurling in Ireland.

8. False. Although the ball can be thrown from player to player, it must be kicked into the goal in order for the goal to count.

9. D. Rugby Union. Brian Driscoll is the Irish national rugby union team's most capped player, with a total of 133 international appearances to his name. Fly-half Johnny Sexton is Ireland's top points scorer, having scored an

incredible 1,108 points in his international career, from 2009 to 2023. Both are also former captains of the Irish national rugby team.

10. B. Floyd Mayweather, Jr. Billed as "The Money Fight," the bout recorded the second-highest pay-per-view buy rate in history, with both fighters rumored to have earned more than $100 million for their involvement. Although scheduled for 12 rounds, Mayweather—who was at the time the undefeated 11-time five-division boxing world champion—won by a knockout in the tenth round.

11. D. –14 under par. McIlroy had already made history the day before by achieving a US Open round score of –13 under par but bettered it by one the following day. On his way to winning the Open competition outright, he set the record for the lowest second-round 36-hole total in the contest's history (131, finishing the second day –11 under par), and then the lowest third-round 54-hole total in the contest's history (199, finishing the third day –14 under par). He then went into the final round already holding an eight-stroke lead over his closest rival and finished the contest with a final score of 268—the lowest four-round 72-hole score in US Open history. Having also achieved the rare feat of finishing all four US Open rounds under par, McIlroy ended the contest with a staggering par score of –16, a full eight points clear of the second-place finisher, Australia's Jason Day, who ended on –8 under par.

12. C. 3. Whether above or below the crossbar, the ball must pass between the two uprights for the goal to count at all.

13. C. Athletics. Having won gold at the world championships in Gothenburg, Sweden, in 1995, O'Sullivan took the silver

medal in the women's 5,000m at the Sydney Olympic Games in 2000.

14. A. "The fastest sport in the world." The phrase refers to the fact that the ball in a game of hurling is almost continuously played at immensely high speeds, struck through the air from player to player, and so is almost always off the ground.

DID YOU KNOW?

The sport of camogie is referenced in Samuel Beckett's play Waiting For Godot.

THE FOOTBALLER WHO (ALMOST) BECAME PERSON OF THE YEAR

Every year, the renowned American publication *Time* magazine names its Person (or sometimes People) of the Year.

Past winners have included such history-shaping figures as Harry Truman, Winston Churchill, Pope John Paul II, Queen Elizabeth II, and even pop superstar Taylor Swift. But back in 1999, with the millennium fast approaching, *Time* launched a new initiative to name its official Person of the Century: The figure from the past 100 years of history and culture who had shaped the 1900s more than anyone else.

Understandably, the nominations included some astonishingly important and powerful figureheads, among them Mahatma Gandhi, President Franklin D. Roosevelt, Rosa Parks, and even Soviet leader Vladimir Lenin. In a somewhat shortsighted move, however, *Time* opened the nominations for their Person of the Century poll to the public. This being around the time that the internet was becoming truly available worldwide, it did not take long for some people to take advantage of the loophole in *Time*'s poll that allowed readers to nominate whomever they wished.

As a result, an email chain went around the Republic of Ireland, urging everyone who received it to nominate unassuming Irish footballer Ronnie O'Brien for the coveted title of *Time*'s Person of the Century.

O'Brien had had a stellar soccer career in Ireland as a youngster, eventually becoming part of the Republic of Ireland youth team that won the Under-16 European Championships in 1998. He subsequently made the move to Middlesbrough FC, an English league club, before being released early from his contract there to sign with the much-admired Italian soccer team Juventus in 1999 — all before his 20th birthday.

O'Brien's meteoric rise from a lowly teenage Irish soccer star to playing for one of the biggest clubs in the world was understandably the source of considerable pride among Irish fans. It was they who ultimately spearheaded the plan to have him win *Time*'s Person of the Millennium. The plan almost worked too: as the email encouraging people to cast their votes for O'Brien was sent on to more and more people across the Republic of Ireland, O'Brien crept up the ranks until he was eventually at one point leading the poll outright!

Alas, the editors of *Time* saw fit to alter the rules of the poll halfway through voting and stepped in to declare that "whimsical candidates will not be considered." As a result, O'Brien's name was removed from the voting — and someone else named Albert Einstein ended up winning the much-coveted title instead!

CHAPTER 14
IRELAND IN THE MOVIES II

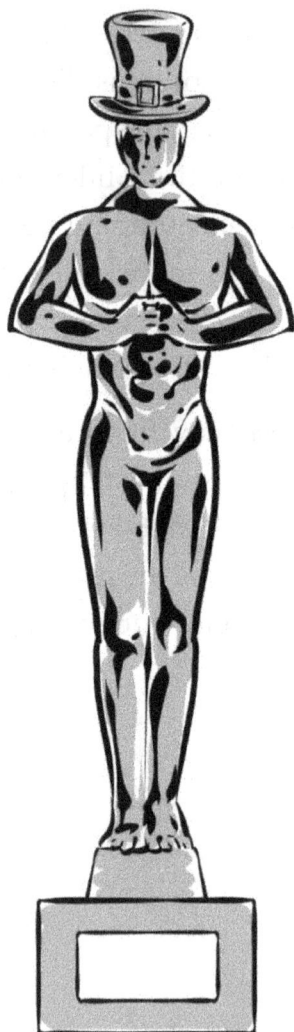

Time for one second and final round of questions about Irish cinema. Once again, we're covering several decades of moviemaking and Hollywood history here—and looking at Oscar-winning dramas, niche comedies, movie musicals, and one of the biggest movie franchises in film history!

1. Who replaced Irish actor Richard Harris in the role of Hogwarts headmaster Dumbledore in the *Harry Potter* movies, following his death in 2002?

    a. Ian McKellen
    b. Patrick Stewart
    c. Michael Gambon
    d. Derek Jacobi

2. In 2024, Irish actor Paul Mescal played the lead role in the long-awaited sequel to what Oscar-winning blockbuster?

    a. *The Sixth Sense*
    b. *Catch Me If You Can*
    c. *Saving Private Ryan*
    d. *Gladiator*

3. Which Irish actor starred opposite Tom Cruise in the 2002 sci-fi thriller *Minority Report*?

    a. Cillian Murphy
    b. Colin Farrell
    c. Barry Keoghan
    d. Brendan Gleeson

4. In the 2015 movie *Brooklyn*, starring Saoirse Ronan as a young Irish woman who emigrates to 1950s New York, which legendary actress played the landlady, Mrs. Kehoe, who runs the boarding house at which she lives?

a. Judi Dench
b. Julie Walters
c. Helen Mirren
d. Helena Bonham Carter

5. Who directed the 1991 musical comedy-drama *The Commitments*, about a working-class soul and rock 'n' roll band in Dublin?

a. Sam Mendes
b. Danny Boyle
c. Mike Leigh
d. Alan Parker

6. Which visiting professor at Hogwarts did Irish Oscar-nominee Brendan Gleeson play in the *Harry Potter* movies?

a. Remus Lupin
b. "Mad-Eye" Moody
c. Quirinus Quirrell
d. Gilderoy Lockhart

7. Which Oscar-nominated Irish actor played the revolutionary leader Michael Collins in the 1996 biopic of the same name?

a. Daniel Day-Lewis
b. Michael Fassbender
c. Liam Neeson
d. Stephen Rea

8. Directed by Joel Schumacher, who starred as journalist Veronica Guerin in the 2003 biopic of the renowned journalist whose investigation of the Dublin drug scene led to her murder in 1996?

a. Cate Blanchett
b. Nicole Kidman

c. Naomi Watts

d. Natalie Portman

9. What 2022 Irish movie set on a remote Irish island starred Colin Farrell, Brendan Gleeson, Kerry Condon, and Barry Keoghan—all of whom were nominated for Oscars for their performances?

    a. *The Banshees of Inisherin*

    b. *Calm With Horses*

    c. *Delinquent Season*

    d. *The Killing of a Sacred Deer*

10. Which of these movies was NOT directed by Irish filmmaker Neil Jordan?

    a. *The Crying Game*

    b. *Interview with the Vampire*

    c. *Mona Lisa*

    d. *In the Name of the Father*

11. After starring in the television drama series *Chernobyl* and *Fargo*, Irish actress and singer Jessie Buckley made her Hollywood breakthrough in the 2021 movie, *The Lost…*what?

    a. *Mother*

    b. *Aunt*

    c. *Daughter*

    d. *Sister*

12. In 1989, Kenneth Branagh received his first ever Oscar nominations for his role in and direction of an adaptation of which Shakespeare play?

    a. *Macbeth*

    b. *As You Like It*

c. *Henry V*

d. *The Tempest*

13. Which 2015 drama was adapted for the big screen by the Irish-born author of the book on which it was based, Emma Donoghue?

   a. *Ex Machina*

   b. *Bombshell*

   c. *Room*

   d. *The Hours*

14. Who directed the acclaimed 2006 Irish Civil War drama *The Wind That Shakes the Barley*?

   a. Steven Spielberg

   b. Ken Loach

   c. Richard Attenborough

   d. Tom Hooper

SOLUTIONS

1. C. Michael Gambon. Richard Harris played Professor Albus Dumbledore in both of the first two *Harry Potter* movies (2001's *Harry Potter and the Sorcerer's Stone* and 2002's *Harry Potter and the Chamber of Secrets*) before Sir Michael Gambon—who, like Harris, was also born in Ireland!—took over the role for the remainder of the series.

2. D. *Gladiator*. Once again directed by Ridley Scott, *Gladiator II* also starred Pedro Pascal, Denzel Washington, and Connie Nielsen.

3. B. Colin Farrell. Based loosely on a 1956 Philip K. Dick novella by the same name, *Minority Report* was one of the year's biggest hits and grossed over $350 million at the 2002 box office.

4. B. Julie Walters. Walters was nominated for Best Supporting Actress at the BAFTAs for her performance in the film, while Saoirse Ronan went on to achieve her second Oscar nomination (and her first in the Best Actress category).

5. D. Alan Parker. The movie went on to be nominated for an Oscar and six BAFTAs.

6. B. "Mad-Eye" Moody. Professor Alastor "Mad-Eye" Moody was the Defense Against the Dark Arts teacher in Harry Potter's fourth year at Hogwarts, as recounted in the fourth book and film in the series, *Harry Potter and the Goblet of Fire*.

7. C. Liam Neeson. With a budget of $25 million, at the time *Michael Collins* was one of the most expensive movies ever made in Ireland—but was also one of the most acclaimed of the year. It was awarded the Golden Lion at the 1996 Venice

Film Festival, where Neeson also took the award for Best Actor.

8. A. Cate Blanchett. Cate Blanchett would go on to be nominated for a Golden Globe for her performance.

9. A. *The Banshees of Inisherin*. In all, the movie was nominated for nine Academy Awards, including Best Actor, Best Supporting Actress, two Best Supporting Actor nods, and the awards for Best Picture, Director, and Screenplay.

10. D. *In the Name of the Father*. Neil Jordan was nominated for an Oscar for his direction of *The Crying Game* in 1992 — while *In the Name of the Father*'s director Jim Sheridan was also nominated for Best Director two years later, in 1994.

11. C. *Daughter*. The feature directorial debut of actress Maggie Gyllenhaal, *The Lost Daughter* also starred Olivia Colman (who was also nominated for an Oscar for her role) and Dakota Johnson.

12. C. *Henry V*. Belfast-born Branagh — who was named one of Ireland's greatest-ever actors by the *Irish Times* in 2020 — has since become the first person in Oscar history to be nominated for awards in seven different categories!

13. C. *Room*. Emma Donoghue was nominated for an Oscar for her screenplay, while the film's star, Brie Larson, won the Academy Award for Best Actress.

14. B. Ken Loach. Winner of the Palme d'Or at the 2006 Cannes Film Festival and Ken Loach's highest-grossing movie, *The Wind That Shakes the Barley* starred Cillian Murphy and Pádraic Delaney as two brothers who find themselves fighting on opposite sides of the Irish Civil War.

DID YOU KNOW?

Ireland's largest cinema is the Cineworld complex on Parnell Street, Dublin. It has 17 screens and was the first cinema in the British Isles to offer movies in 4DX—using moving seats, wind fans, and even spritzes of water to give cinemagoers an immersive movie-watching experience!

THE IRISHMAN WHO DESIGNED THE OSCAR

For such a relatively small country, Ireland has a remarkably good track record at the Academy Awards. In the awards' near-century of history, there have been over 100 Irish nominees and more than 20 Irish wins—including statuettes for the likes of Kenneth Branagh, Cillian Murphy, Martin McDonagh, and three for Daniel Day-Lewis. However, Ireland's greatest-ever Oscar winner—and nominee, for that matter—had a lot more to do with the Academy Awards than anyone else can lay claim to, and likely always will.

Although born in New York in 1890, Cedric Gibbons' family was half-Irish. He grew up in the city with an Irish-born father, Austin, who worked as an architect, and an American-born mother, Veronica. The family moved to Manhattan when Cedric was still a child, and after studying at the Art Students League of New York, in 1911 he joined his father's architectural practice as a draftsman. Cedric seemed destined for a career in New York design—but at the outbreak of World War I, he was drafted into the US Navy Reserves, and after the conflict was over, relocated to California.

There, Gibbons found work at the renowned Goldwyn Studios and, in 1924, began a long professional relationship with MGM, working behind the scenes in their movie studios. It was while working for MGM that Gibbons became one of the founding members of the newly formed Academy of Motion Picture Arts and Sciences. In 1928, when the Academy decided to introduce an annual awards ceremony to honor recent achievements in motion pictures, they called on Gibbons to design the statuette that would be bestowed on the Academy's honorees. Gibbons, ultimately, was responsible for designing the Oscar!

That being said, Gibbons did not cast or sculpt the Oscar statuette himself; rather, he only provided its designs and blueprints on paper. Neither was it his idea to nickname the Academy Award the "Oscar": the Hollywood legend Bette Davis used to claim that the name was her idea (as the rear of the statue supposedly reminded her of her husband, Harmon Oscar Nelson!). Another story claims Academy librarian Margaret Herrick renamed the award (because Gibbons' design supposedly looked like her Uncle Oscar). Nevertheless, the size and shape of the Oscar statuette is all thanks to Cedric Gibbons—and once the awards were instituted, he quickly went on to amass quite a collection of them!

Besides his work for the Academy, Gibbons was a cinematic art director, and over the next three decades of his career, he would provide behind-the-scenes design work for some of Hollywood's most successful and memorable movies—among them, *The Great Ziegfeld* (1936), *The Wizard of Oz* (1939), *The Picture of Dorian Gray* (1945), *Annie Get Your Gun* (1950), *Quo Vadis* (1951), and *Blackboard Jungle* (1955). Incredibly, Gibbons was nominated for the Academy Award for Best Art Direction for every single one of those movies—as well as a further 33 more, for a career total of 39 Academy Award nominations! And, even more incredibly, he won no less than 11 Oscars in total throughout his career, taking the statuette he designed home with him for his work on films such as *Pride and Prejudice* (1940), *Gaslight* (1944), *Little Women* (1949), *An American in Paris*

(1951), and Marlon Brando's renowned adaptation of Shakespeare's *Julius Caesar* (1953).

Gibbons died in Los Angeles in 1960, at the age of 70. His extraordinary Oscar haul remains the greatest of any Irish movie-maker — but his efforts in creating the actual Oscar statuette itself set his work and his victories aside from everyone else in Hollywood history!

CHAPTER 15
IRISH FOLKLORE II

Time for one final test of your knowledge of Irish folklore, with this last set of questions covering everything from mischievous sprites to perilous superstitions.

1. According to tradition, what is a leprechaun's job when not guarding his pot of gold at the bottom of a rainbow?

    a. Baker
    b. Carpenter
    c. Ironmonger
    d. Cobbler

2. *Samhain* is an ancient Celtic festival roughly corresponding to what other holiday?

    a. Christmas
    b. Easter
    c. Halloween
    d. Valentine's Day

3. According to tradition, which of these is a simple but effective way of protecting yourself against Irish fairies?

    a. Putting a hat on
    b. Wearing something yellow
    c. Removing your shoes
    d. Turning an item of clothing inside out

4. In Irish folklore, which of these would be most likely to be inhabited by a mischievous sprite called a *clurichaun*?

    a. School
    b. Barroom
    c. Barn
    d. Bank

5. In the popular Irish folk tale *Feather o' my Wing*, what kind of creature claims to be a handsome prince who has been transformed into an animal by a magical sorceress?

    a. Magpie
    b. Badger
    c. Caterpillar
    d. Hedgehog

6. "Thunderbolt" Gibbons was a renowned 19th-century Irish outlaw. According to folklore, how did he receive his nickname?

    a. Because he was notably hot-tempered.
    b. Because he was proficient in sailing through tempests.
    c. Because he was known for traveling so rapidly.
    d. Because he was born during a thunderstorm.

7. *The Happy Prince and Other Tales* and *A House of Pomegranates* are collections of fairy stories and folk tales written by which famous Irish writer?

    a. James Joyce
    b. Oscar Wilde
    c. Samuel Beckett
    d. WB Yeats

8. A traditional Irish "fairy tree" is typically what kind of tree?

    a. Oak
    b. Yew
    c. Willow
    d. Hawthorn

9. What is the worst day on which to hold a wedding, according to an old Irish superstition?

   a. Sunday
   b. Tuesday
   c. Friday
   d. Saturday

10. An Irish *merrow* best resembles what other fantastical creature?

   a. Werewolf
   b. Mermaid
   c. Vampire
   d. Zombie

11. "Saturday's flit is a short sit" is an old Scots and Irish proverb, superstitiously warning against doing what on a Saturday?

   a. Marrying
   b. Drinking
   c. Cooking
   d. Moving house

12. The legendary Irish hero Finn MacCool had a pet dog named Bran. According to legend, Bran was the ancestor of all dogs of what breed?

   a. Highland terrier
   b. Wolfhound
   c. Bulldog
   d. Beagle

13. In ancient Ireland, it was once believed that people were more likely to be abducted by fairies in what month of the year?

    a. January
    b. May
    c. August
    d. December

14. What bizarre old tradition is sometimes done on wedding days in Ireland?

    a. Tying the groom's shoelaces together
    b. Passing the married couple under a horse
    c. Breaking the wedding cake over the bride's head
    d. Locking the priest in the church bell tower

SOLUTIONS

1. D. Cobbler. Where the tradition of the leprechaun being a cobbler or shoemaker comes from is unknown. One explanation, however, is that rather than help other people mend their shoes, the leprechaun is habitually seen fixing his own shoes—because he spends so much time fleeing from people trying to steal his gold and soon wears out his boots!

2. C. Halloween. Samhain begins on the evening of October 31 and lasts until the following day. For that reason, the name *Samhain* is also the Irish name for the month of November.

3. D. Turning an item of clothing inside out. Exactly how or why this method was supposed to ward off malevolent Irish fairies, or *sidhe*, is unknown, but you can allegedly protect yourself against fairies by inverting any item of clothing, no matter how big or small—from your shirt or coat to a sock or a glove!

4. B. Barroom. Clurichauns are mischievous leprechaun-like creatures whose love of drink often leads them to haunt wine cellars, breweries, pubs, and bars.

5. A. Magpie. Other versions of this tale have a black crow in place of a magpie, but in all variants of the story, a bird lands on a rich gentleman's arm claiming to be a prince. The youngest of the gentleman's daughters is wooed by the magpie and ends up releasing the prince from his enchantment.

6. C. Because he was known for traveling so rapidly. Gibbons was a "Whiteboys" captain—one of a band of outlaws who challenged and outwitted unscrupulous landowners.

According to tradition, Gibbons was known for conducting vicious nighttime raids on rack-renters, then expertly and swiftly fleeing capture.

7. B. Oscar Wilde. Published in 1888 and 1891, the two collections include stories such as "The Nightingale and the Rose," "The Star-Child," and "The Young King."

8. D. Hawthorn. Fairy trees are lone trees that stand in the center of open fields. Often local people protect the trees — and the spirits that supposedly use them — by laying stone circles around their bases.

9. B. Tuesday. The best day for a wedding, conversely, is said to be Wednesday!

10. B. Mermaid. A *merrow*, or Irish *murúch*, is a half-man or - woman and half-fish creature. Unlike other mermaids, however, according to some stories, an Irish merrow can only swim underwater thanks to the wearing of a magical cap.

11. D. Moving house. A flit is a swift movement from one place to another, so this saying is warning against "flitting" or moving somewhere new on a Saturday — because, as a consequence of the bad luck involved, you will end up being in the new home for only a "short sit," i.e., a short time. The tradition is so deeply established, especially among older people in Ireland, that one study in 2003 found that even hospital patients in Ireland dislike being sent home on the weekend and would rather remain in the hospital until the following week!

12. B. Wolfhound. According to legend, all Irish wolfhounds the world over are the descendants of MacCool's hound Bran.

13. B. May. According to superstition, the veil that separates our world from that of the fairies disappears on May Day Eve and May Day itself, making this period the most likely for a person to be abducted.
14. C. Breaking the wedding cake over the bride's head. According to an old marriage tradition, it is good luck to break a slice of the wedding couple's cake over the bride's head as she is carried across the threshold of her new home. For the tradition to work, however, it has to be the bride's new mother-in-law who holds the cake, with the ceremonial break thereby guaranteeing that the two will remain close friends and never argue for the entire duration of the bride's marriage.

DID YOU KNOW?

Although seven is a popular lucky number the world over, the number three is also seen as a sign of good luck in Ireland because it is the number of leaves on a traditional Irish shamrock.

KNOCKING OVER YOUR CHAIR, AND OTHER IRISH SUPERSTITIONS

Ireland is a land of history and folklore, and a great many of the superstitions people like to believe today—such as counting magpies, tossing spilled salt over your shoulder, and avoiding breaking mirrors for fear of seven years of bad luck—have evolved from old Celtic and Irish traditions.

Among the many other Irish superstitions that have not caught on, however, is the notion that knocking your chair over backward when you stand up is a guarantee of bad luck to come (as well as your own clumsiness!). It is a tradition in Ireland, too, that when making a circular soda bread, it should be scored or cut into a cross shape to help ward off the devil.

A festive superstition in Ireland, meanwhile, claims that a candle should be allowed to keep burning in the window of a home throughout the Christmas period. If at any time the flame were to burn out or be blown out, the household would be cursed with bad luck for the year to come. It was also once considered bad luck to gift anything sharp to a close friend at Christmastime, as the blade might risk "cutting" the friendship asunder.

According to Irish tradition, bad luck can also be predicted using various bodily signs. An itchy nose, for instance, is said to mean that someone nearby wants to have an argument with you. An itchy left hand, meanwhile, means that you have money on your way—while an itch on your right hand implies the opposite!

CONCLUSION

And with that final deep dive into the bizarre traditions and superstitions of Ireland, your *Ultimate Irish Challenge* is complete!

We do hope you have enjoyed the last hundred or so pages of all things Ireland and Irish—from poets, bards, music, and melodies to sports stars, Oscar-winners, bridges, and wars. We've covered a host of subject areas here and wandered back through more than a thousand years of history (and 100 years of moviemaking!).

So how did you do? A true Irish expert would no doubt have excelled here, but did you find yourself sailing to victory or having the odd stab in the dark (or, for that matter, taking a peek at the solutions!)? Not to worry if you're guilty of that, of course—there were some very tricky questions here, and with so many subjects on the table, there was bound to be something that was a little out of your wheelhouse!

Easy or difficult, the main thing here is that you had fun while trying to answer these questions—and even if you did resort to glancing at the answers, hopefully, you learned a thing or two about the fascinating, welcoming, and endlessly varied country of Ireland. *Sláinte!*

www.ingramcontent.com/pod-product-compliance
Lightning Source LLC
Chambersburg PA
CBHW051735020426
42333CB00014B/1328